AHFG

· All Hazard Field Guide ·

ISBN-13: 978-1456448240

ISBN-10: 1456448242

LCCN: 2010918627

Printed in the United States of America

All Hazard Field Guide

A Responder's Handbook using the National Incident Management System's Incident Command System

by

Tim Deal — Chuck Mills — Mike Deal

— CONTENTS —

— Figures & Tables —

OPERATIONAL PLANNING CYCLE

INCIDENT COMMANDER

INCIDENT COMMANDER GUIDES

UNIFIED COMMAND

COMMAND STAFF

COMMAND STAFF GUIDES

OPERATIONS SECTION

OPERATIONS SECTION CHIEF GUIDES

PLANNING SECTION

PLANNING SECTION CHIEF GUIDES

SITUATION UNIT LEADER GUIDES

DOCUMENTATION UNIT LEADER GUIDES

DEMOBILIZATION UNIT LEADER GUIDES

RESOURCES UNIT LEADER GUIDES

LOGISTICS SECTION

LOGISTICS SECTION CHIEF GUIDES

FINANCE/ADMINISTRATION SECTION

AREA COMMAND

BRANCH TACTICAL PLANNING

INTRODUCTION

The idea for this All Hazard Field Guide (AHFG) came from responders who were customizing their Incident Command System (ICS) field guides and incident management handbooks. They would add checklists and other memory joggers to their books to better suit their needs. We thought, if responders are customizing the field guides and handbooks, then current publications are missing information that the responders find valuable, and we should try to fix that.

This All Hazard Field Guide - A Responder's Handbook using the National Incident Management System's Incident Command System is our attempt to take the traditional field guide and incident management handbook to a new level.

We combed through existing material on ICS and checked with fellow responders to see what they were adding to their response field guidance. We wanted to create a field guide that not only reminds you what to do, but how to do it. For example, Chapter 9 of our AHFG is titled Operations Section and it covers the responsibilities of key Operations Section positions.

What makes the AHFG unique is the following chapter, Chapter 10, Operations Section Chief Guides. Here you will find 12 job-aids such as the Tactics Meeting Preparation Guide that outlines the basic steps in developing a tactical plan (the "how to" piece). For all key ICS positions, we have added aids to help you accomplish your responsibilities.

In a lot of ways, the All Hazard Field Guide is a companion to our first book *Beyond Initial Response*. Like our first book, you will find checklists and graphics throughout the field guide that are there to assist you in carrying out your ICS position-specific responsibilities. In addition, we have left plenty of room for you to add your own notes so that you can expand on the information that we have provided.

The All Hazard Field Guide is easy to read and easy to use. It is designed for all hazard incidents and puts more information in your hands. It is a useful guide, regardless of incident size or complexity, and is an important reference for any emergency responder. We hope that you will find this AHFG valuable.

Sincerely,

Chuck Mills

Chuck Mills —

Coauthor — *Beyond Initial Response — Using the National Incident Management System's Incident Command System*

COMMON RESPONSIBILITIES
&
UNIT LEADER RESPONSIBILITIES

Common Responsibilities

The following list is applicable to all personnel in the ICS organization.

1. Receive assignment from your agency, including:
   - Job assignment
   - Brief overview of type and magnitude of incident.
   - Resource order number and request number/ travel authorization
   - Travel instructions, including reporting location and reporting time
   - Any special communications instructions (e.g., communications while in travel status, radio frequency)

2. Prepare to deploy
   - If available, monitor incident-related information from media, internet, social networking, etc.
   - Assess personal equipment readiness for specific incident and climate (e.g., medications, money, computer, medical record). Maintain a checklist of items and possibly a personal go-kit
   - Inform others of where you are going and how to contact you
   - Review your duties outlined in this field guide
   - Take advantage of available travel to rest prior to arrival

3. Upon arrival at the incident, check in at the designated check-in location. (If you are instructed to report directly to a tactical assignment, check in with the Division/Group Supervisor or the Operations Section Chief) Check-in may be found at any of the following locations:
   - Incident Command Post (ICP)
   - Incident Base
   - Staging Areas
   - Helibases
   - Camps

4. Receive briefing from immediate supervisor

5. Agency representatives from assisting or cooperating agencies report to the Liaison Officer (LOFR) at the ICP after check-in

6. Acquire work materials

7. Follow organizational code of ethics

8. Participate in incident management team (IMT) meetings and briefings as appropriate

9. Ensure compliance with all safety practices and procedures. Report unsafe conditions to the Safety Officer (SOF)

10. Supervisors shall maintain accountability for their personnel with regard to their exact location(s), personal safety, and welfare at all times, especially when working in or around incident operations

11. Supervisors shall organize and brief subordinates

12. Know your assigned communication methods and procedures for your area of responsibility and ensure that communication equipment is operating properly

13. Communicate clearly and use ICS terminology (no codes) in all radio communications

14. Complete forms and reports required of the assigned position and ensure proper disposition of incident documentation as directed by the Documentation Unit

15. Ensure all equipment is operational prior to each work period

16. Report any signs/symptoms of extended incident stress, injury, fatigue or illness for yourself or coworkers to your supervisor

17. Brief shift replacement on ongoing operations when relieved at operational periods or when rotating out

18. Respond to demobilization orders and brief subordinates regarding demobilization

19. Prepare personal belongings for demobilization

20. Return all assigned equipment to appropriate location

21. Complete demobilization check-out process before returning to home base

22. Participate in after-action activities as directed

23. Carry out all assignments as directed

24. Upon demobilization, notify Resources Unit Leader (RESL) at incident site and home unit of your safe return

Unit Leader Responsibilities

In ICS, a number of the Unit Leader's responsibilities are common to all functions within the ICS organization. Common responsibilities of Unit Leaders are listed below. These <u>will not</u> be repeated in Unit Leader Position Checklists in subsequent chapters.

- *Review Common Responsibilities in this chapter*
- *Upon check-in, receive briefing from Incident Commander, Section Chief, Branch Director, Supervisor, off going Unit Leader as appropriate*
- *Participate in incident meetings and briefings, as required*
- *Determine current status of unit activities*
- *Determine resource needs*
- *Order additional unit staff, as appropriate*
- *Confirm dispatch and estimated time of arrival of staff and supplies*
- *Assign specific duties to staff and supervise staff*
- *Develop and implement accountability, safety and security measures for personnel and resources*
- *Supervise demobilization of unit, including storage of supplies*
- *Provide the Supply Unit Leader with a list of supplies to be replenished*
- *Maintain unit records, including Unit Log (ICS-214)*
- *Individual responders may want to maintain personal log of actions, decisions and events*
- *Carryout all assignments as directed*

OPERATIONAL PLANNING CYCLE, MEETINGS, BRIEFINGS, AND THE ACTION PLANNING PROCESS

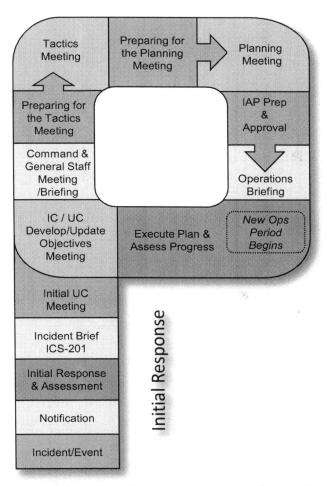

Refer to position specific chapter guides for additional information on your role in the planning process.

Initial Response and Assessment

The period of initial response and assessment occurs in all incidents. Short-term responses, which are small in scope and/or duration (e.g., a few resources working in one operational period), are often coordinated using only an ICS-201 Incident Briefing Form.

Planning P — Incident Brief

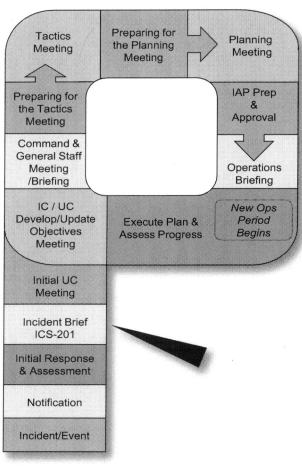

"Planning P"

Incident Briefing (ICS-201)

The ICS-201 is an excellent tool for the initial Incident Commander to help organize and manage the initial response. It was designed to document initial response actions such as: current incident situation, incident objectives, actions taken, incident organization, and resources requested and assigned to the incident.

The ICS-201, Incident Briefing Form functions as the Incident Action Plan (IAP) for the initial response and remains in effect and continues to be updated until the response ends or the Planning Section generates the incident's first IAP. It also provides a historical record of the initial response actions.

In addition to documenting response information and being used during transfer of command, the ICS-201 is a good method for providing newly arriving responders with a quick overview of the incident so that they can better understand the situation.

In the event that the initial Incident Commander will be handing off command of the incident, an ICS-201 formatted briefing provides for the orderly transfer of command when an incoming Incident Commander (IC)/Unified Command (UC) prepares to assume responsibility for the incident.

Use the following agenda to help guide your briefing.

Facilitator:	Current IC/UC or PSC (if available)
Attendees:	Prospective IC/UC; Command and General Staff, as available

Incident Briefing Agenda (Use the ICS-201 as an outline):

1. Current situation (note territory, exposures, safety concerns, etc.; use map/charts)
2. Initial objectives and priorities
3. Current and planned actions
4. Current on-scene organization
5. Resource assignments
6. Resources enroute and/or ordered
7. Facilities established
8. Incident potential

"Incident Briefing ICS-201 Meeting Agenda"

Planning P — Initial Unified Command Meeting

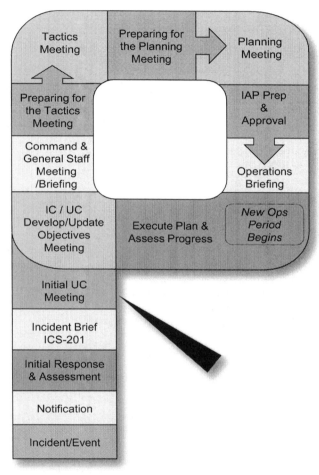

"Planning P"

Initial Unified Command Meeting

The initial meeting provides UC officials with an opportunity to discuss and concur on important issues prior to the Unified Command Objectives Meeting. The meeting should be brief and all important decisions and direction should be documented. Prior to the meeting, Unified Commanders should have an opportunity to review and prepare to address the agenda items. The results of this meeting will help to guide the overall response efforts.

Use the following agenda to help guide your meeting.

Facilitator: UC member or PSC (if available)

Attendees: ICs that comprise the UC, deputy ICs and DOCL

Initial Unified Command Meeting Agenda:

1. Meeting brought to order, cover ground rules and review agenda

2. Validate makeup of newly formed UC, guided by Chapter 6 criteria

3. Clarify UC roles and responsibilities

4. Review agency policies

5. Negotiate and agree on Key Decisions which may include:

   a. UC jurisdictional boundaries and focus (Area of Responsibility (AOR)

   b. Name of incident

   c. Overall response organization, including integration of assisting and cooperating agencies

   d. Location of Incident Command Post (if not already identified) and other critical facilities, as appropriate

   e. Operational period length/start time and work shift hours

   f. Best-qualified Operations Section Chief and Deputy OSC

   g. Other key Command and General staff assignments and technical support as needed

6. Summarize and document key decisions

"Initial UC Meeting Agenda"

Planning P – UC Objectives Meeting

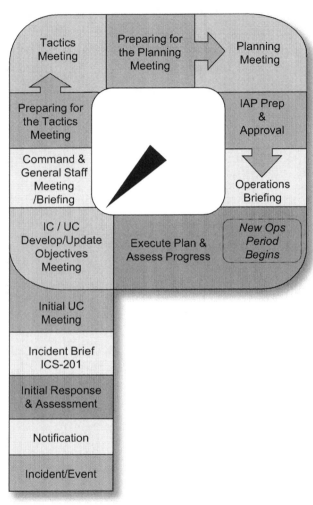

"Planning P"

UC Objectives Meeting

The UC will set response priorities, identify any limitations and constraints to the response, develop incident objectives and establish guidelines for the IMT to follow. For recurring meetings, all products will be reviewed and updated as needed. Products resulting from this meeting, along with decisions and direction from the Initial UC meeting, will be presented at the Command and General Staff Meeting.

Chapter 4 contains examples of key decisions, incident priorities, incident objectives and constraints and limitations.

Chapter 5 has examples of staff assignments that you may want members of the IMT to focus on.

Note: If you are the sole Incident Commander for the incident, this "step" in the planning process is time for you to gather your thoughts before meeting with your Command and General Staff.

Use the following agenda to help guide your meeting.

Facilitator: PSC

Attendees: UC Members; Selected Command and General Staff, SITL and DOCL

UC Objectives Meeting Agenda:

1. PSC brings meeting to order, conducts roll call, covers ground rules and reviews agenda

2. Review and/or update key decisions

3. Develop or review/update response priorities, limitations and constraints

4. Develop or review incident objectives

5. Develop or review/update key procedures which may include:

   a. Managing sensitive information

   b. Information flow

   c. Resource ordering

   d. Cost sharing and cost accounting

   e. Operational security issues

6. Develop or review/update tasks for Command and General Staff to accomplish

7. Review, document and/or resolve status of any open actions

8. Agree on division of UC workload

9. Prepare for the Command and General Staff Meeting

"UC Objectives Meeting Agenda"

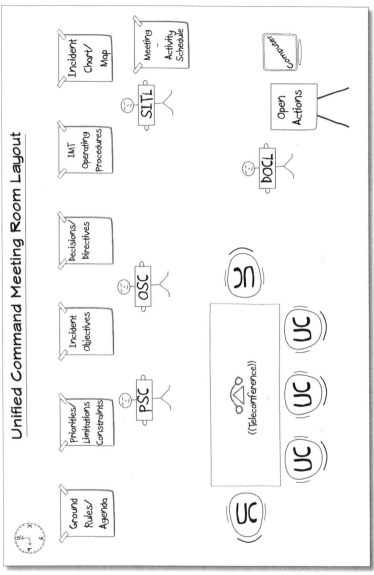

"Unified Command Meeting Room Layout"

Planning P — Command and General Staff Meeting

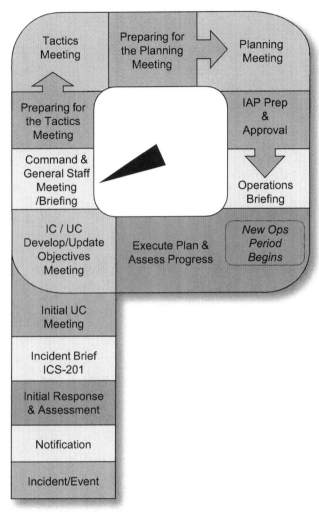

Tactics Meeting

Preparing for the Planning Meeting

Planning Meeting

Preparing for the Tactics Meeting

IAP Prep & Approval

Command & General Staff Meeting /Briefing

Operations Briefing

IC / UC Develop/Update Objectives Meeting

Execute Plan & Assess Progress

New Ops Period Begins

Initial UC Meeting

Incident Brief ICS-201

Initial Response & Assessment

Notification

Incident/Event

"Planning P"

Command and General Staff Meeting

At the Command and General Staff Meeting, the IC/UC will present their decisions and management direction to the Command and General (C&G) Staff members. This meeting should clarify and help to ensure understanding among the core IMT members on the decisions, objectives, priorities, procedures and functional assignments (tasks) that the UC has discussed and reached agreement on.

Follow-on Command and General Staff Meetings will cover any changes in Command direction, review open actions and review status of assigned tasks.

Use the following agenda to help guide your meeting.

Facilitator: PSC

Attendees: IC/UC Members, Command and General Staff, SITL, and DOCL

Command and General Staff Meeting Agenda:

1. PSC brings meeting to order, conducts roll call, covers ground rules and reviews agenda

2. SITL conducts situation status briefing

3. IC/UC
   a. Provides comments
   b. Reviews key decisions, priorities, constraints and limitations (if new or changed)
   c. Discusses incident objectives
   d. Reviews key procedures (if new or changed)
   e. Assigns or reviews functional tasks/open actions

4. PSC facilitates open discussion to clarify priorities, objectives, assignments, issues, concerns and open actions/tasks (each C&G member will be called upon for any questions, concerns or issues)

5. IC/UC provides closing comments

"Command and General Staff Meeting Agenda"

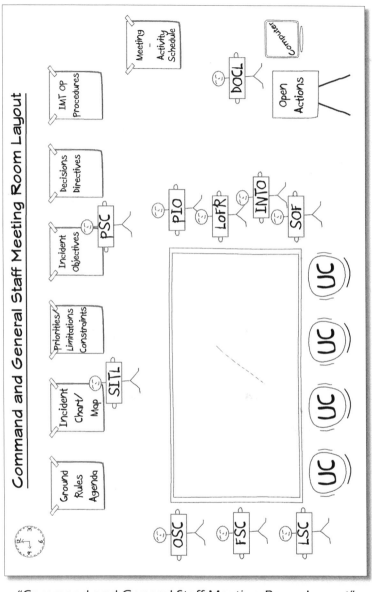

"Command and General Staff Meeting Room Layout"

Planning P — Preparing for the Tactics Meeting

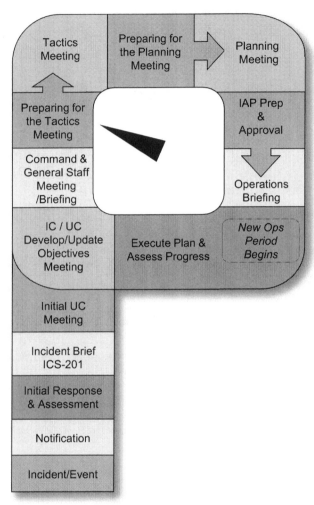

"Planning P"

Preparing for the Tactics Meeting

During this phase of the Operational Planning Cycle, the OSC and PSC begin the work of preparing for the upcoming Tactics Meeting. They review incident objectives to determine those that are the OSC's responsibility and they consider Command priorities.

The OSC and PSC also document strategies and tactics to meet assigned objectives and draft an Operational Planning Worksheet (ICS-215) and an Operations Section organization chart for the next operational period.

In addition, the SOF should begin to develop the Incident Action Plan Safety Analysis Worksheet (ICS-215a). The PSC should facilitate/support this process to the greatest extent possible to ensure that the information to be presented in the Tactics Meeting is organized and accurate.

Planning P — Tactics Meeting

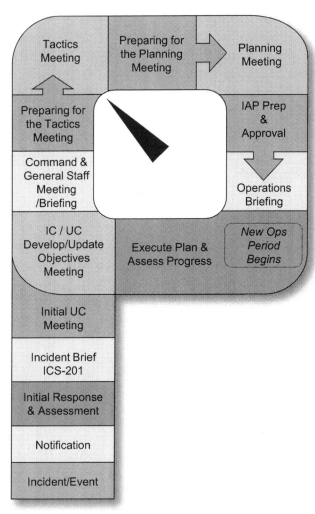

"Planning P"

Tactics Meeting

This meeting allows for operational input needed to support the IAP. The OSC will present strategies using the draft Operational Planning Worksheet (ICS-215). The proposed Operations Section organization will also be presented by OSC. The SOF will present the draft Incident Action Plan Safety Analysis Worksheet (ICS-215a). OSC/PSC will solicit input of attendees in order to refine these draft products for full staff approval at the Planning Meeting.

Use the following agenda to help guide your meeting.

Facilitator: PSC

Attendees: OSC, LSC, RESL, SITL, SOF, DOCL, COML, THSP (as needed), FSC (optional)

Tactics Meeting Agenda:

1. PSC brings meeting to order, conducts roll call, covers ground rules and reviews agenda

2. SITL reviews the current & projected incident situation

3. PSC reviews incident operational objectives and ensures accountability for each

4. OSC reviews response strategies

5. OSC reviews and/or completes the Operational Planning Worksheet (ICS-215) which addresses:
   - Work assignments
   - Resource commitments
   - Contingencies
   - Needed support facilities, i.e., Staging Areas

6. OSC reviews and/or completes Operations Section organization chart

7. SOF reviews and/or completes the Incident Action Plan Safety Analysis Worksheet (ICS-215a) and identifies and resolves any critical safety issues

8. LSC discusses and resolves any logistics issues

9. PSC validates connectivity of tactics and operational objectives

"Tactics Meeting Agenda"

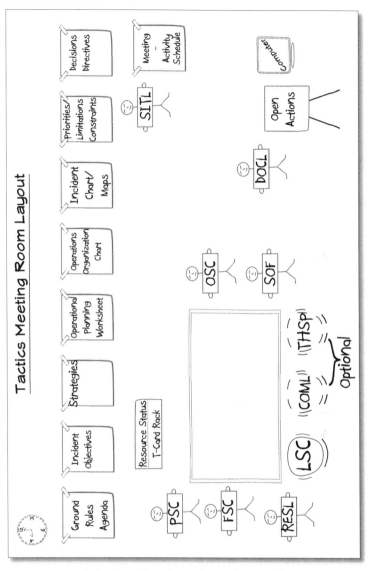

"Tactics Meeting Room Layout"

Planning P — Preparing for the Planning Meeting

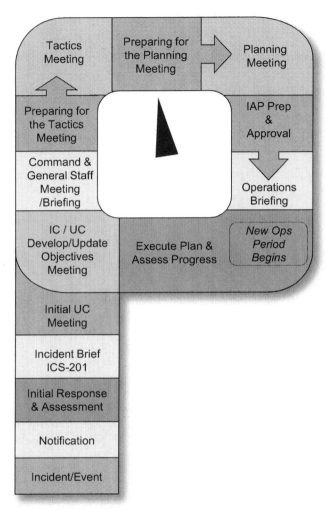

"Planning P"

Preparing for the Planning Meeting

The Command and General Staff prepare for the upcoming Planning Meeting. The PSC ensures the information used or discussed in the Planning Meeting is prepared and ready for presentation during the meeting.

Planning P — Planning Meeting

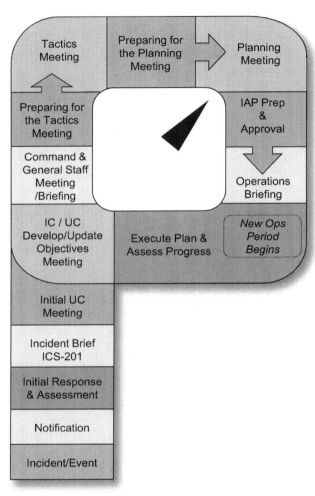

"Planning P"

Planning Meeting

The point of this meeting is to provide an overview of the tactical plan to achieve Command's (IC/UC) current direction, priorities and objectives. The OSC will present the proposed plan to the Command and General Staff for review and comment. The meeting also provides the opportunity for the Command and General Staff to discuss and resolve any issues and concerns prior to assembling the IAP. After review and updates are made, Planning Meeting attendees commit to supporting the plan. Command must give provisional approval of the plan before the meeting adjourns.

Use the following agenda to help guide your meeting.

Facilitator: PSC

Attendees: IC/UC, Command Staff, General Staff, SITL, DOCL and THSP (as required)

Planning Meeting Agenda:

1. PSC brings meeting to order, conducts roll call, covers ground rules and reviews agenda

2. IC/UC provides opening remarks

3. SITL provides briefing on current situation, resources at risk, weather forecast and incident projections

4. PSC reviews Command's incident priorities, decisions and objectives

5. OSC provides briefing on current operations, an overview of the proposed plan including strategy, tactics/work assignments, resource commitments, contingencies, Operations Section organization structure and support facilities, i.e., Staging Areas continued...

...cont'd

6. PSC reviews proposed plan to ensure that Command's priorities and operational objectives are met

7. PSC reviews and validates responsibility for any open actions/tasks and management objectives

8. PSC conducts "round robin" of Command and General Staff members to solicit their final input and commitment to the proposed plan:

   a. LSC covers transportation, communications and supply updates and issues

   b. FSC covers fiscal issues

   c. SOF covers safety issues

   d. PIO covers public affairs and public information issues

   e. LOFR covers interagency issues

   f. INTO covers intelligence issues

9. PSC requests Command's provisional approval of the plan as presented. IC/UC may provide final or closing comments

10. PSC issues assignments to appropriate IMT members for developing IAP support documentation along with deadlines

"Planning Meeting Agenda"

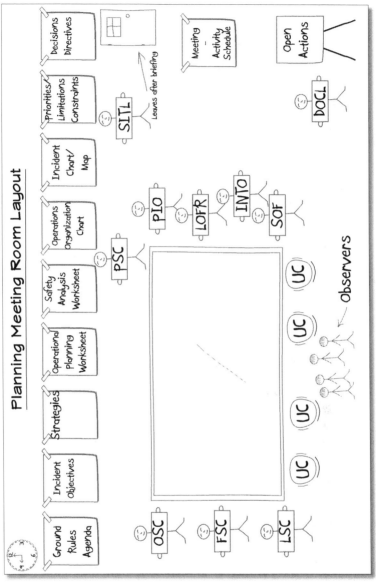

"Planning Meeting Room Layout"

Planning P — IAP Preparation and Approval

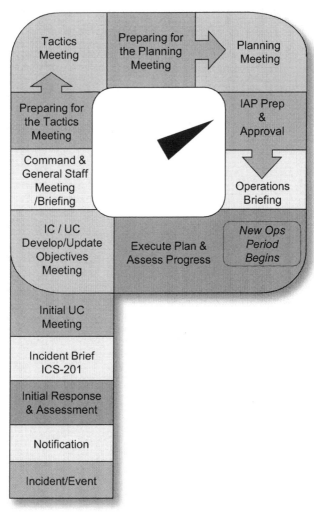

"Planning P"

Incident Action Plan Preparation and Approval

IMT members must immediately complete the assigned tasks/products that are needed for inclusion in the IAP. These products must meet the deadline as set by the PSC so that the Planning Section can assemble the IAP components. The deadline must be early enough to permit timely IC/UC review, approval, and duplication of sufficient copies for the Operations Briefing and for other IMT members.

IAP Common Components (Primary Responsibility)

1. Incident Objectives (ICS-202) — (RESL)
2. Organization List/Chart (ICS-203/207) — (RESL)
3. Assignment List (ICS-204) — (RESL)
4. Communication Plan (ICS-205) — (COML)
5. Medical Plan (ICS-206) — (MEDL)
6. Site Safety Plan (ICS-208) — (SOF)
7. Incident Map/Chart — (SITL)
8. Weather — (SITL)

Optional Components (use as pertinent):

1. Air Operations Summary (ICS-220) — (AOBD)
2. Demobilization Plan — (DMOB)
3. Transportation Plan — (GSUL)
4. Decontamination Plan — (THSP)
5. Waste Management or Disposal Plan — (THSP)
6. Other Plans and/or documents, as required

"IAP Common Components"

Planning P — Operations Briefing

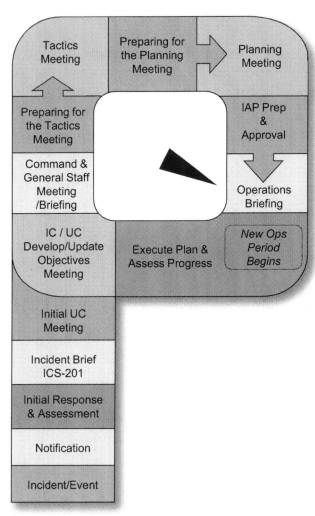

"Planning P"

Operations Briefing

This briefing presents the IAP to the Operations Section oncoming shift supervisors. After this briefing has occurred and during shift change, off-going supervisors should be interviewed by their relief and by the OSC in order to validate IAP effectiveness.

Use the following agenda to help guide your briefing.

Facilitator: PSC

Attendees: IC/UC, Command and General Staff, Branch Directors, Division/Group Supervisors, Task Force/Strike Team Leaders (if possible), Unit Leaders, others as appropriate

Operations Briefing Agenda:

1. PSC opens briefing, covers ground rules, agenda and takes roll call of Command and General Staff and Operations personnel required to attend

2. PSC goes over general contents of the plan, reviews IC/UC objectives and makes any required changes to the IAP (i.e., pen-and-ink changes)

3. IC/UC provides remarks

4. SITL conducts situation briefing along with predictions

5. OSC discusses current response actions and accomplishments

6. OSC briefs Operations Section personnel

7. LSC covers transportation, communications and supply updates

8. FSC covers fiscal issues

9. SOF covers safety issues, PIO covers public affairs and public information issues, LOFR covers interagency issues and INTO covers intelligence issues

10. PSC solicits final comments and adjourns briefing

"Operations Briefing Agenda"

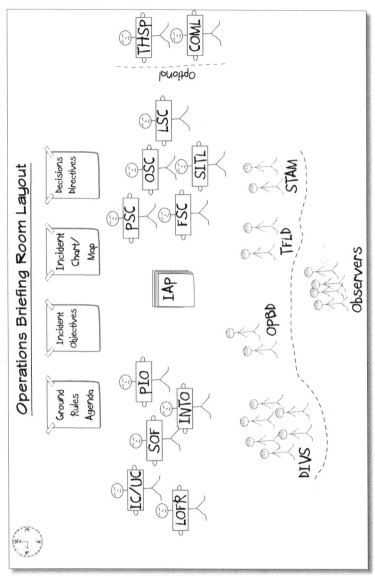

"Operations Briefing Room Layout"

Planning P — Execute Plan & Assess Progress

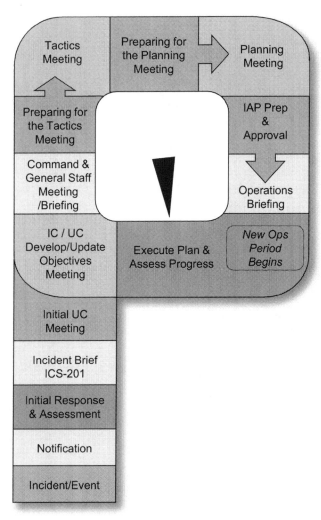

"Planning P"

Execute Plan & Assess Progress

Assessment is a continuous process to help adjust current operations and help plan for future operations. Following the briefing and shift change, all Command and General Staff will review the incident response progress and make recommendations to the IC/UC in preparation for the next IC/UC Objectives Meeting. This feedback/information is continuously gathered from various sources, including Field Observers, responder debriefs, stakeholders, etc. The IC/UC should encourage Command and General Staff to get out of the ICP and view firsthand the areas of the incident that they are supporting.

Other meetings may occur during the ICS Planning Process. Some of these are summarized below.

Special Purpose Meetings

Special Purpose meetings are most applicable to larger incidents requiring an Operational Planning Cycle, but may also be useful during the Initial Response Phase.

Business Management Meeting

The purpose of this meeting is to develop and update the Business Management Plan for finance and logistical support. The agenda could include: documentation issues, cost sharing, cost analysis, finance requirements, resource procurement, and financial summary data. Attendees normally include: FSC, COST, PROC, LSC, and DOCL.

Agency Representative Meeting

This meeting is held to update Agency Representatives and ensure that they can support the IAP. It is conducted by the LOFR, and attended by Agency Representatives. It is most appropriately held shortly after the Planning Meeting in order to present the plan (IAP) for the next operational period. It allows for minor changes in the event that the plan does not meet Agency Representatives expectations.

Media Briefing

This meeting is normally conducted at the Joint Information Center (JIC). Its purpose is to brief the media and the public on the most current and accurate facts. It is set up by the PIO, moderated by a UC spokesperson, and features selected spokespersons. Spokespersons should be prepared by the PIO to address anticipated issues. The briefing should be well-planned, organized, and scheduled to meet media's needs.

Demobilization Planning Meeting

This meeting is held to gather functional requirements from the IC/UC and Command and General Staff that would be included in the incident Demobilization Plan. Functional requirements would include: safety, logistics, and fiscal considerations and release priorities that would be addressed in the plan. Attendees normally include: IC/UC, OSC, PSC, LSC, FSC, LOFR, SOF, INTO, PIO and DMOB. The DMOB then prepares a draft Demobilization Plan to include the functional requirements and distributes it to IC/UC and Command and General Staff for review and comment.

INCIDENT COMMANDER

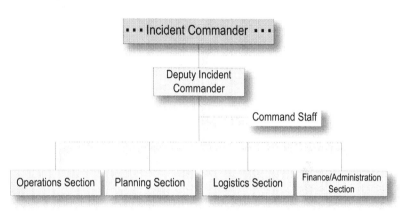

"Incident Commander in relation to the Command and General Staff"

The Incident Commander (IC) is responsible for the overall management of the incident. Guides to help you, the IC, carryout your responsibilities can be found in Chapter 5.

On many incidents, the command activity is conducted by a single Incident Commander. If working in a Unified Command, take a look at Chapter 6.

Note — Consider the use of deputies if the incident is complex and will take time to bring under control.

The Major Responsibilities of the IC are:

a. Review Common Responsibilities in Chapter 2

b. If relieving another IC, get a thorough briefing (see Chapter 21 "Transfer of Command")

c. Determine incident objectives and general direction for managing the incident

d. Establish incident priorities

e. Identify potential limitations and/or constraints

f. Establish an Incident Command Post

g. Establish an appropriate organization

h. Brief Command Staff and Section Chiefs

i. Determine when to shift from reactive to proactive response posture

j. Ensure planning meetings and briefings are scheduled as required

k. Approve and authorize the implementation of the IAP

l. Ensure that adequate safety and security measures are in place

m. Coordinate activity for all Command and General Staff

n. Ensure that coordination and communications with external entities are established and maintained

o. Coordinate with key people and officials

p. Approve requests for additional resources or for the release of resources

q. Keep agency administrator informed of incident status

r. Ensure that critical information reporting requirements are met

s. Approve the use of trainees and volunteers

t. Authorize release of information to the news media and stakeholders

u. Ensure Incident Status Summary (ICS 209) is completed and forwarded to appropriate higher authority

v. If required, ensure that individual performance evaluations are conducted

w. Order the demobilization of the incident when appropriate

x. Maintain Unit Log (ICS-214)

Command's Direction

Incident Commander(s) are responsible for providing direction and guidance to the Incident Management Team (IMT). ICs must analyze the overall requirements of the incident and determine the most appropriate direction for the management team to follow during the response. This is accomplished by making key decisions, setting priorities, identifying limitations and developing response objectives for the incident.

Remember that the Incident Commander manages the team and the team manages the incident.

Examples of Key Decisions

- Incident name
- Organizations/agencies that will be represented in Unified Command
- Integration of other supporting and cooperating organizations/agencies
- Support facilities and locations (ICP, Base, JIC etc)
- Operational period and hours of operation
- Issuing delegation of authority to staff
- Identifying critical information reporting process
- Managing sensitive information
- Managing external influences
- Resource requesting/ordering, cost sharing, and cost accounting
- Operational security issues
- Staffing of primary positions (OSC and Deputy)
- Developing incident response priorities
- Identifying IMT procedures/functions
- Determining how command will function

Examples of Incident Priorities

- Safety/security and welfare of responders and the public
- Reduce threat to Homeland Security
- Minimize adverse impact on the environment
- Restoration of the transportation infrastructure/ and commerce
- Minimize further loss of property
- Investigation and apprehension of those responsible
- Reduce/prevent further threat/attack

Establishing Incident Objectives

The incident objectives that you set for the response will be used to guide the actions of every responder who comes to assist in the response. Objectives are critical to the response effort. If objectives are unclear, your team will have to guess at what it is you want and may not accomplish what you want. If objectives are too narrow, your team will not have the flexibility necessary to adapt to a changing situation.

Objectives are not always easy to develop, but there's a speedy way to evaluate whether the ones you created are on the right track. To evaluate your objectives ask yourself the following questions:

1. Is your objective <u>Specific</u>? (Is the objective focused enough that responders know what you want done?)

2. Is your objective <u>Measurable</u>? (Can you measure progress toward completion of the objective?)

3. Is your objective <u>Attainable</u>? (Do you understand the situation clearly enough that the objective isn't impossible to accomplish given the constraints of resources, weather, geography, etc?)

4. Is your objective <u>Realistic</u>? (Can your objective be accomplished?)

5. Is your objective <u>Time Sensitive</u>? (Whenever possible, place a time frame for when the objective should be accomplished (e.g., 11:00 AM 31 December)

The SMART model may be difficult to achieve in the early phases of the response, but as the response matures the use of SMART is a great way to evaluate your objectives.

Examples of Incident Objectives

The following are example objectives that can help you in developing your response objectives. The list is not inclusive, and you will have to tailor your objectives to the situation to which you are responding.

Safety Objectives

- Provide for the safety, security and welfare of citizens and response personnel
- Provide for the safety and security of responders and maximize the protection of public health and welfare
- Identify safety and risk management factors and monitor for compliance for both the public and responders
- Establish a stop-work protocol
- Develop a process for responder injury/accident reporting
- Conduct Operational Risk Assessment and ensure controls are in place to protect responders and the public
- Ensure that incident support facilities are safe and secure
- Ensure that safety is appropriately addressed in the IAP and support plans

Search and Rescue Objectives

- Locate and evacuate all injured personnel
- Evacuate victims to medical transfer areas or facilities once rescued
- Establish medical triage and transport to hospital
- Conduct urban search and rescue
- Locate, triage, treat, and transport trapped victims to advanced medical care facilities

Firefighting Objectives

- Contain, extinguish and overhaul fire
- Ensure that exposures are protected to prevent further spread of fire
- Ensure coordination with law enforcement for scene security
- Identify cause of fire
- Ensure close coordination with entities initiating potential victim evacuation
- Coordinate with public works to ensure that an adequate water supply is maintained
- Monitor structures to determine their stability
- Ensure backup rescue team available for confined space entry
- Ensure that an effective responder accountability system is established and maintained
- Ensure that an appropriate decontamination capability is readily available

Security, Law Enforcement, and Investigation Objectives

- Implement procedures to ensure a coordinated effort is in place for investigations, evidence collection, and forensics

- Implement security awareness measures, including evaluation of changes in incident effects, response conditions, and secondary threats, including potential targeting of first responders and contamination

- Implement measures to isolate, contain and stabilize the incident, including establishment and adjustment of security perimeters

- Establish use of force policies for responders from different agencies

- Establish incident security plan, including identification badges and other scene-control measures

- Investigate cause of incident

- Establish and continue enforcement of safety/security zones

- Identify and implement witness recovery location(s)

- Request FAA implement air space restrictions and monitoring for compliance

Radiation Objectives

- Develop and implement radiological protective action guides
- Identify source and radioactive isotope
- Conduct monitoring operations to determine the extent of contamination
- Develop radiological waste disposal plan
- Develop plan to mitigate spread and possible re-suspension of radioactive contamination
- Implement measures to isolate, contain, and stabilize the source of radiation
- Conduct monitoring operations to validate plume projections
- Conduct assessment of radiological contamination to determine impact on the environment
- Develop initial plume projections
- Develop and implement first responder radiation dose limits
- Develop plan for handling contaminated corpses
- Develop and implement population monitoring plan
- Develop and implement radiation decontamination plan
- Establish and implement incident site control zones (hot zone, warm zone, cold zone)
- Ensure coordination of technical data between all stakeholders (collection, analysis, storage, and dissemination)
- Develop and implement evacuation plan

Oil Spill/HAZMAT Release Objectives

- Initiate actions to control the source and minimize the release

- Determine oil/hazmat fate and effect (trajectories/plume modeling) identify threats to populated and environmentally sensitive areas Develop strategies for protection and conduct mitigation

- Contain and recover released/spilled material (Hazmat/Oil)

- Conduct an assessment and initiate cleanup efforts

- Remove product from impacted areas

- Conduct efforts to effectively contain, clean up, recover and dispose of released/spilled product

- Identify locations for the temporary storage and long-term disposal of waste from the incident

Environmental Objectives

- Protect environmentally sensitive areas, including wildlife and historic properties

- Identify and maximize protection of environmentally sensitive areas

- Initiate environmental cleanup activities

- Identify threatened species and prepare to recover and rehabilitate injured wildlife

- Investigate the potential for, and if feasible, use alternative technologies to support response efforts

- Develop and implement a long-term monitoring and recovery plan

Public Works Objectives

- Install and maintain barriers to help law enforcement secure any identified safety/security zones

- Conduct stability assessments on critical infrastructure in the impact zone

- Provide public works resources in support of both tactical and logistics requirements

- Work with public utilities to determine short- and long-term effects on services provided to the impacted population

- Remove debris to reestablish and maintain ingress and egress to the affected area. If necessary, determine alternate routes for ingress and egress

- Coordinate with the IMT for debris removal and access to waste sites

- Assist community-based organizations to establish and maintain evacuation shelters

- Assist emergency communications network for the affected area for both responders and affected population

Public Health Objectives

- Initiate and maintain health assessment program for both responders and affected population

- Assist the IMT to determine and establish safety/security zones

- Work with the IMT to evaluate the effect of responder exposure and recommend appropriate personal protective equipment

- Recommend and supervise mass quarantine of exposed population

- Recommend and provide inoculation measures to contain spread of the sickness/illnesses

- Support the IMT public outreach initiative (media messaging and publication development and distribution)

- Provide a conduit between the IMT, CDC and World Health Organization

- Provide technical guidance to IMT personnel related to overall public health issues

- Act as liaison between the IMT and the hospital system

- Conduct water and air sampling to determine exposure levels

- Assess public health impacts and recommend mitigation measures

- Conduct mental health assessments and recommend treatment for affected population

- Evaluate the need for, and provide critical incident stress management for responders and the public

- Inspect incident support facilities from a health perspective and recommend corrective measures as needed

Management Objectives

- Provide Critical Incident Stress Management (CISM) services to responders

- Establish a Family Assistance Program and assign a coordinator

- Manage a coordinated interagency response effort that reflects the makeup of Unified Command

- Establish an appropriate IMT organization that can effectively meet the initial and long term challenges required to mitigate the incident

- Identify all appropriate agency/organization mandates, practices, and protocols for inclusion in the overall response effort

- Identify and minimize social, political and economic adverse effects

- Implement a coordinated response with other responding entities including EOC(s) and the JFO

- Evaluate all planned actions to determine potential impacts on social, political and economic entities

- Identify competing response activities to ensure that they are closely coordinated

- Identify and establish incident support facilities to support interagency response efforts

- Keep the public, stakeholders and the media informed of response activities

- Ensure appropriate financial accounting practices are established and followed

- Ensure internal/external resource ordering procedures are established and followed

- Establish an incident documentation system

- Establish an appropriate structure to facilitate communications with stakeholders and agency/organization coordination facilities

Constraints and Limitations

Incident Management Team members will undoubtedly be faced with a number of issues that will adversely impact the management of the incident. Identifying these issues will allow the IMT to find alternative approaches to managing the incident, given the constraints and limitations. Some examples of common constraints and limitations:

- Limited resources
- Interagency communications
- Extent of contamination
- Operations in contaminated environment
- Decontamination
- Special needs population
- Evidence preservation/crime scene integrity
- Multiple hazards
- Large scale evacuation
- Media
- Responder dose rates
- Secondary devices
- Weather and work environment
- Rugged terrain
- Vegetation type
- Civil disturbances
- Political influences
- Competing incidents
- Financial resources
- Economic impacts
- Site security/perimeter

INCIDENT COMMANDER GUIDES

This chapter is designed to help you, the Incident Commander perform your duties and responsibilities.

- ✓ *Initial Incident Commander Actions Checklist*
- ✓ *ICS Planning Process*
- ✓ *IC Develop/Update Objectives Meeting*
- ✓ *Command and General Staff Meeting (C & G Meeting)*
- ✓ *Examples of staff assignments for the C & G Meeting*
- ✓ *Preparing for the Planning Meeting*
- ✓ *Planning Meeting*
- ✓ *Guidance when reviewing the Incident Action Plan*
- ✓ *Operations Briefing*
- ✓ *Execute Plan and Assess Progress*
- ✓ *IMT Operating Procedures Topics*
- ✓ *IMT evaluation*
- ✓ *Working under an Area Command*
- ✓ *Top Five Things to Remember*

Incident Commander Initial Actions Checklist

If you are the initial Incident Commander, use the checklist below to help remember the critical management actions that you should take after arriving on-scene.

- ☐ *Assess the incident situation; ensure safety of public and responders*
    - ☐ *Use all of your senses (sight, smell, hearing, etc.)*
- ☐ *Verify situation against initial report of the incident and communicate findings*
- ☐ *Establish command as initial Incident Commander*
- ☐ *Determine who is on-scene*
    - ☐ *Other responders*
    - ☐ *Spontaneous volunteers*
- ☐ *Redirect resources based on initial observations*
- ☐ *Identify limitations and constraints*
- ☐ *Begin to conduct a detailed assessment and react as appropriate*
    - ☐ *Identify life-safety and security issues*
    - ☐ *Evaluate potential threat to population*
    - ☐ *Identify immediate environmental issues*
    - ☐ *Identify potential threats to property*
- ☐ *Ensure that incident evidence is protected*
- ☐ *Determine need to subdivide incident into workable management units*
    - ☐ *Divisions, Groups, etc.*
- ☐ *Document decisions and actions*

ICS Planning Process

As the Incident Commander, you are an integral part of the ICS Planning Process. The following pages provide some guidance on your role in each "step" in the Process.

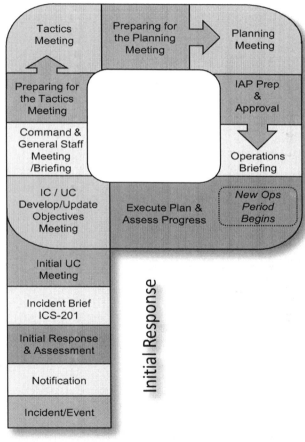

"Planning P"

IC/UC Develop/Update Objectives Meeting

□ *Determine priorities for the incident (e.g., evacuate injured, secure area, and suppress the fire)*

□ *Determine the incident response objectives (The objectives form the foundation of the IAP. A poor foundation means a poor plan). Are the objectives:*

    □ *Specific*

    □ *Measurable*

    □ *Attainable*

    □ *Realistic*

    □ *Time Sensitive*

□ *Determine the operational period – The operational period is the period of time that an Incident Action Plan (IAP) is designed to cover. For example, if you want 12-hour-long operational periods, an IAP will have to be developed twice a day. Take into account:*

    □ *Pace of the operations*

    □ *Rate of change in incident situation*

    □ *Weather or other criteria and trends that impact ability to work*

    □ *Safety and well-being of responders*

□ *Establish an incident organization that is capable of meeting initial and long-term challenges required to mitigate the incident*

    □ *Is your span-of-control within limits*

    □ *Did you consider the need for a Deputy*

□ *Identify and select incident support facilities*

    □ *Incident Command Post*

    □ *Base*

    □ *Staging Areas*

    □ *Camps*

- Ensure scene integrity and evidence preservation

- Identify constraints and limitations (e.g., will respond during daylight hours only and without aircraft support)

- Identify Incident Management Team Operating Procedures for the incident (e.g., organization's protocols for dealing with next-of-kin notifications)

- Make any other key decisions that will impact the overall response

Command and General Staff Meeting

Some items you want to cover during the meeting include:

- *Your priorities (e.g., the highest priority is the protection of structures)*
- *Present any limitations and/or constraints*
- *Review the incident objectives for the next operational period so your management team can begin work on the IAP*
- *Define the hours of work and operational period*
- *Identify staffing requirements*
    - *Who will be the Operations Section Chief*
- *Any directions (e.g., ensure that tactical operations are planned to minimize impact to wildlife)*
- *Clarify any staff roles and responsibilities*
- *Expectations of the team for staff communications*
- *Identify staff assignments that you want done and who is responsible (see following)*

Examples of Staff Assignment for the C & G Meeting

One of your responsibilities during the Command and General Staff Meeting is to identify and assign tasks to the members of the Command and General Staff. The needs of the incident will help you identify the tasking that needs to be done, but if it has been awhile since you have participated in a C & G Meeting, the examples of various tasks listed below might be a good place to start.

Safety Officer

- Develop site safety plan for on-scene operations and support facilities and monitor for compliance
- Work with the COML to ensure effective communications plan is developed and monitored for compliance
- Ensure coordination with the MEDL for medevacs, investigation and injury reporting
- Keep command informed of any accidents and injuries
- Keep command informed of any safety decisions that will adversely impact operations

Public Information Officer

- Keep command informed of any potential political, social, and economic impacts
- Develop a media strategy (press briefings, media releases)
- Ensure law enforcement sensitive and classified information is not publicly disseminated
- Provide Command with talking points for VIP, media and public meetings
- Ensure all incident personnel are briefed on appropriate media protocols

Intelligence Officer

- Identify critical intelligence needs and develop intelligence flow plan and brief the Incident Management Team (IMT)
- Ensure Command is briefed on all intelligence reports
- Be the central point of coordination for all interagency intelligence organizations (e.g., Joint Terrorism Task Force)
- Screen intelligence information for operational security/security sensitive information

Liaison Officer

- Develop a plan to ensure communications and coordination with appropriate stakeholders and submit draft plan to command for review and approval
- Ensure coordination with the PIO and Situation Unit Leader in developing talking points for VIP and community meetings

Planning Section Chief

- Assess the need for Technical Specialists to support incident operations

- Ensure all off-site information reporting (e.g., situation reports) is approved by Command prior to release

- Brief the IMT on document control system, including handling, accounting, disposal and storing procedures for incident documentation

- Establish and post a meeting/situation briefing schedule

- Have the Incident Action Plan ready for Command's review and approval one-hour prior to the Operations Briefing

- Develop Information Management Plan to address how information is gathered, processed and disseminated

- Assess the need for Critical Incident Stress Management services

Operations Section Chief

- Transition current operations toward accomplishing new direction and objectives as much as possible

- Immediately notify Command of new developments that will adversely effect accomplishment of stated objectives

- Address alternative strategies for accomplishing objectives

- Advise Command of any major resource and specialized equipment (e.g., air monitoring) shortfalls

- Immediately advise Command of any interagency issues that adversely effect accomplishment of incident objectives

Finance/Administration Section Chief

- Provide Command with a daily cost estimate summary and identify high cost items

- Establish a claims system and brief IMT on process

- Notify Command of any cost limitations and constraints that may adversely effect response efforts

Logistics Section Chief

- Develop and brief IMT on internal/external resource ordering process and monitor for compliance

- Ensure that appropriate security is established at all incident support facilities

- Develop a plan for credentialing responders and all other personnel requiring access to the incident

- Evaluate need for, and establish as necessary, secure and non-secure communications for both internal and external communication traffic

- Whenever possible, maximize use of information technology to enhance incident management processes and development of work products

General

- Build a functional organization that effectively and efficiently carries out Command's directives

- Maximize interagency integration, cooperation and coordination

- Resolve all performance and conduct issues promptly and report unresolved issues immediately to Command

Preparing for the Planning Meeting

- Check in with the Operations Section Chief (OSC) to find out how the current operations are going and whether there are any concerns about ongoing or future operations

- Talk with the Planning Section Chief (PSC) to see how the team is functioning

- Meet with the Logistics Section Chief to discuss any issues in regard to resources and supplies to support the incident

- Spend time with the Safety Officer and find out if there are any concerns

Planning Meeting

Here are some items that you will need to do to support the meeting:

- *Provide opening remarks (remember that the focus is on the future, so keep your comments forward-leaning)*
    - *Discuss any changes, deletions, or additions to the original incident objectives that you gave your team earlier*
    - *Discuss where you see progress and where improvements can be made*
- *Make sure that the tactical plan that the OSC has briefed follows your directions and the incident objectives have been properly addressed*
    - *Are you comfortable that the responder and public safety risks are properly balanced with the priorities you've established*
    - *Is the OSC-proposed organization adequate to meet the needs of the incident*

- Provide any necessary further guidance and resolve any issues that come up

- Give provisional approval of the proposed IAP

- Agree on a time when the Planning Section Chief will be ready to give you a written IAP for your review and final approval

Guidance When Reviewing the Incident Action Plan

When reviewing the IAP, look for the following:

- Are the incident objectives and priorities accurately recorded?

- Have safety concerns been adequately addressed?

- Does the Communications Plan address command, tactical, and support communications needs?

- Are the assignments for each Division, Group, Staging Area, etc. clear and concise?

- Can Logistics realistically support the plan?

- Have stakeholder concerns been adequately addressed?

- Has intelligence and security been considered?

- Is the Medical Plan useable?

- Does the IAP support the Delegation of Authority and any other direction received from superiors?

Operations Briefing

Your role in this briefing is to:

- *Provide a leadership presence*
- *Provide overall guidance*
- *Provide motivational remarks*
- *Emphasize your response philosophy*
    - *Teamwork*
    - *Safety*

Execute Plan and Assess Progress

Some things to consider as you assess incident operations:

- *Review progress of assigned tasks with the OSC*
- *Receive periodic situation briefings*
- *Review work progress*
- *Identify changes that need to be made during current and future operational periods*
- *Ensure that the organization you have in place is adequate for what you're facing*

Incident Management Team (IMT) Operating Procedures

When operating in a multi-agency response operation with different agencies filling Command and General Staff positions, it is important to establish a set of IMT operating procedures so that everyone is working under the same expectations. Some of the topics that might be covered in the IMT operating procedures are listed below. The list is not inclusive as each incident presents its own challenges.

- Information Management – internal and external
- Cost sharing and accountability
- Acquiring appropriate logistics support (e.g., water, food)
- Performance evaluation
- Management of Intelligence products
- Management of classified information
- Managing incident specific critical information
- Screening and identification for responders
- Collection and preservation of evidence
- Managing incident investigation
- External briefing schedule (e.g., EOC, Agency Administrator, Area Command)
- Managing incident documentation (e.g., photos, e-mails)
- Establishing briefing threshold for keeping Command informed (e.g., in what situations does Command want to be immediately informed)
- Resource ordering process
- Establishing a responder "code of conduct"

Incident Management Team Evaluation

As either the sole Incident Commander or a member of the Unified Command, it is important to take a few minutes and evaluate the effectiveness of your Incident Management Team (IMT). This is especially true if the IMT is comprised of members from different organizations that may not have a history of working together in a high operational tempo environment. The list below should help you conduct a quick evaluation of your team:

- *How is the morale within the different functions and the IMT as a whole?*

- *Are any individual team members showing aggression and/or frustration?*

- *Are scheduled activities, including meetings and briefings carried out according to agreed upon protocols?*

- *Are the Sections and other IMT entities conducting daily meetings?*

- *Are open actions being effectively tracked and closed?*

- *Is information being shared among the team members?*

- *Is off-site reporting on time and accurate?*

- *Is the ICS Planning Process effective and being followed?*

- *Are supervisors (agency administrators) pleased/ displeased with overall team effectiveness?*

- *Are interagency issues effectively resolved and communicated to Command?*

- *Is technology being appropriately used to support the incident and development of the IAP?*

- Does the Operations Section Chief follow the IAP and provide feedback on work accomplishments?

- Are contingencies being implemented as needed?

- Is the staff prepared to participate during meetings and briefings?

- Is there team synergy and cooperation?

- Are status briefings crisp and to the point?

- Does the Planning Section Chief have a handle on the status of resources?

- Are appropriate incident support facilities activated to support operations?

- Are the various IMT functions appropriately staffed to support the incident requirements?

- Are ICS tools being used properly?

- Are work/rest rotations being enforced?

- Are stakeholders satisfied with the response?

Working Under an Area Command

If you find yourself working under an Area Command, you want to ensure that there is good coordination between your Incident Management Team and the Area Command Team. As the on-scene Incident Commander you can help facilitate that coordination by ensuring that Area Command is provided with the following information -

- "Paint" a good situational picture of what your team is facing on the incident

- Your incident objectives

- Include a listing of resources and any other constraints that are limiting the ability to accomplish the objectives

- An assessment of what the impact to the response effort will be if adequate resources are not received (increase suffering and further loss of life)

- Other areas where Area Command could reduce impacts on the Incident Management Team (VIP visits, national media impacts, political pressures, etc.)

- Hours of operation

- Incident priorities

- Agreed upon operating procedures at the local level

- Progress updates along with hindrances

- Political, social, economics, and environmental impacts

- A copy of the Incident Command Post contact directory

- Long-term projections and/or incident potential

- Copy of any maps/charts/building plans of the incident

- Copy of meeting schedule

- Copy of ICS-201, Incident Briefing Form and/or Incident Action Plans

Top Five Things to Remember

"A model for managing complex incidents"

Managing a complex incident presents numerous challenges for you the Incident Commander (IC). It is not hard to lose focus during a demanding response where fatigue and the sheer volume of issues pressing in on you can be daunting. Hopefully, you will never have to face a highly complex incident, but if you do, consider the "Top Five" model.

The "Top Five" model was created by Captains Meredith Austin and Roger Laferriere, US Coast Guard, while responding to the highly complex Deepwater Horizon Oil Spill in the Gulf of Mexico in 2010. The uncontrolled oil spill resulted in millions of gallons of oil entering the Gulf, requiring a response organization of over 40,000 personnel and thousands of vessels. As Incident Commanders, the complexity of the Deepwater Horizon incident required that they prioritize the wide range of issues quickly and efficiently.

The "Top Five" is depicted by a hand. The palm of the hand is you the Incident Commander (or Unified Command), and the fingers represent the five critical areas that must not be overlooked if you want to bring the incident to a safe and successful conclusion.

The guide is simple, and is meant to be a memory jogger for you so that you do not become victim to the tremendous number of lower priority demands placed on you as the Incident Commander. The philosophy behind this model is that if you fail to adequately address any of the five critical areas you risk failure for the entire response.

Here is how the guide works: when you arrive at

the Incident Command Post each morning and are confronted with a long list of items requiring your attention, address them in this order:

(1) People — Issues that are impacting the responders must be addressed first and foremost. Failure to so will directly impact response operations. For example, during the Deepwater Horizon Oil Spill, scores of responders were succumbing to heat stress during initial cleanup operations. Early intervention by the Unified Command ensured timely and adequate controls were in place to avert major heat illnesses or injury.

(2) Incident — Are there adequate resources to execute the objectives? Are the objectives still applicable? After initially arriving on scene to Deepwater Horizon, the Incident Commanders reviewed the objectives and determined the need to increase on-water oil recovery significantly. They tasked the Operations Section with conducting a gap analysis; the result being a request for resources to increase capacity three-fold.

(3) Boss — Everyone has a boss, and bosses need to be kept up-to-date on the incident situation and what the predictions are for bringing the incident under control. Timely and accurate information is essential to the boss so that there are no surprises. During the Deepwater Horizon oil spill response, the Incident Commanders employed assistants acting as aides to help manage their Incident Commander scheduling demands. These assistants were charged with screening phone calls, emails and ensuring that any communications from superiors that were actionable were passed immediately to the Incident Commanders.

(4) Stakeholders — Stakeholders need to be reassured that their concerns are being addressed and that they have an avenue for communicating with the Incident Management Team. During the oil spill, the Incident

Commanders integrated the Governor's Office of Homeland Security representatives from each of the Louisiana parish governments. These personnel, normally charged with managing local emergencies within their jurisdictions, appreciated the overture and became supporters of the overall response effort.

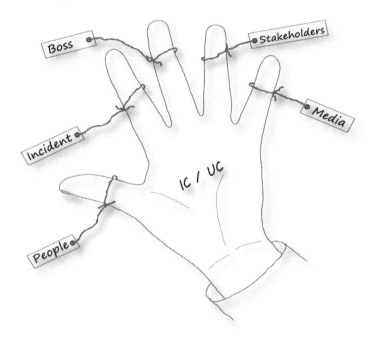

"Top Five Things to Remember"

(5) Media — The media is an important conduit to the public who have a vested interest in the response effort and its impact on the economy and environment. Admiral Thad Allen, the National Incident Commander for Deepwater Horizon, made this one of his top priorities in support of the field Incident Commanders. He was highly effective in instilling confidence in the American public that the Coast Guard was effectively managing the incident.

UNIFIED COMMAND

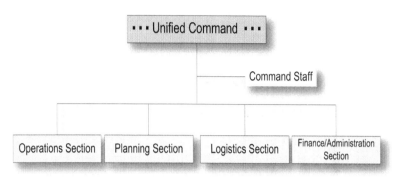

"Unified Command in relation to the Command and General Staff"

Unified Command is about teamwork at the top of the ICS organization. It's about the shared responsibility of command among several Incident Commanders. Unified Command links the organizations responding to an incident and provides a forum for those agencies to make consensus decisions; however, Unified Command is not "decision by committee." Those who are sitting in the Unified Command position are there to command the incident and will have to come together and agree on how to best respond to the incident they're facing. The Unified Command can disagree all they want behind closed doors, but when they emerge and face their management team, they must be united.

The Unified Command may assign Deputy Incident Commander(s) to assist in carrying out the Unified Command's responsibilities.

When Is a Unified Command Necessary

The type of incident, its complexity, and its location will influence whether a UC is established to manage response operations. Some indicators that the response should be managed by a UC include when an incident:

- Crosses geographic boundaries (e.g., two states, Indian Tribal Land)
- Involves various governmental levels (e.g., federal, state, local)
- Involves private industry, or public facilities (e.g., oil company, school)
- Impacts different functional responsibilities (e.g., fire, police, hazardous materials response, emergency medical service)
- Includes different statutory responsibilities (e.g., Federal Land Managers)
- Has some combination of the above

NOTE — Participation in Unified Command occurs without any agency abdicating authority, responsibility, or accountability.

Makeup of the Unified Command

Although there are no limits on how many Incident Commanders can make up the Unified Command, less is always better. There's a lot that is expected of those in the Unified Command and they're operating in a time-critical and mentally demanding environment.

Make every attempt to keep participation on the Unified Command at a manageable level that will enable it to operate in a dynamic environment and rapidly move the response operations forward.

The actual makeup of the Unified Command for a specific incident must be determined on a case-by-case basis taking into account:

- The specifics needs of the incident (e.g., type of incident)
- Determinations outlined in existing response plans
- Decisions reached during the initial meeting of the Unified Command

The makeup of the Unified Command should be flexible and change over time to meet the needs of the incident.

Should you be a member of the Unified Command

To help sort out whether your organization should be included in the Unified Command, use the following as guidance (you should be able to answer 'yes' to all four statements)

1. My organization has jurisdictional authority or functional responsibility under a law or ordinance for the type of incident

2. My organization is specifically charged with commanding, coordinating or managing a major aspect of the response

3. My organization has the resources to support participation in the response organization

4. The incident or response organization impacts my organization's area of responsibility

Unified Command Representatives must have the Authority to

- Agree on common incident objectives and priorities
- Have the capability to sustain a 24-hour, 7-day-a-week commitment to the incident
- Commit agency or company resources to the incident
- Spend agency or organization funds
- Agree on an overall incident response organization
- Agree on the appropriate Command and General Staff position assignments to ensure clear direction for on-scene tactical resources
- Commit to speak with "one voice" through the PIO, LOFR, and through all off-site reporting
- Agree on managing sensitive information and operational security issues
- Agree on logistical support procedures (e.g., resource ordering procedures)
- Agree on cost-sharing and cost accounting procedures, as appropriate
- Agree on constraints/limitations, priorities, decisions and procedures

Unified Command Decisions

Decisions that can be reached by consensus are generally the best, but when consensus cannot be reached on a particular issue, the Unified Command does not come to a screeching halt.

Members of the Unified Command will voice their concerns, but the Incident Commander on the Unified Command that represents the agency with primary jurisdiction and expertise over the specific issue would be deferred to for the final decision.

It is good practice to document significant disagreements among the Unified Command using a decision memo and also note the disagreement in the Unified Command's Decision Log.

<u>Initial Unified Command Meeting</u>

Once the Unified Command (UC) has assumed responsibility for the incident from the initial response Incident Commander, UC members will need to meet quickly to discuss some important issues and make some key decisions.

The Unified Command will be under substantial pressure as members will be working to manage current operations, setting the command team's direction for future activities while simultaneously trying to come together as an effective and efficient team.

The following checklist sets the agenda for the Initial Unified Command Meeting. Use the checklist to guide your UC discussions and ensure that critical decisions are recorded. You're going to have to work quickly to cover the items in the checklist. At this point in the incident response effort, the responders are probably still reacting to events and working on the momentum of the initial response Incident Commander's direction.

Initial Unified Command Meeting Checklist

- ☐ Identify the members of the Unified Command based on the criteria provided previously (Should you be a Member of the Unified Command)

- ☐ Identify jurisdictional and organization priorities and objectives (for each UC member)

- ☐ Present jurisdictional and organizational limitations, concerns, and constraints

- ☐ Establish and agree on acceptable priorities

- ☐ Agree on a basic organizational structure

- ☐ Designate the best qualified and most acceptable Operations Section Chief and Deputy

- ☐ Determine length of the operational period and start time

- ☐ Agree on General Staff personnel assignments in Planning, Logistics, and Finance/Administration

- ☐ Agree on Command Staff assignments, particularly the Public Information Officer who will speak for the UC

- ☐ Determine where Intelligence will be integrated into the response organization

- ☐ Set policy for releasing information to the media and stakeholders

- ☐ Determine the location of the Incident Command Post

- ☐ Determine the need for other incident support facilities e.g., Joint Information Center, Base, evacuation centers

- ☐ Agree on resource-ordering procedures and processes

- ☐ Agree on cost-sharing procedures

- ☐ Determine need to develop any incident management team operating procedures

What if your agency is not represented in Unified Command but is involved in the response effort

Here is how to ensure your organization's concerns or issues are addressed

- Serve as an Agency Representative or company representative with direct access to the Liaison Officer (LOFR).

- Provide stakeholder input to the LOFR (for environmental, economic, social, or political issues).

- Serve as a Technical Specialist in the Planning Section or in other sections as needed.

- Integrate qualified staff into any of the functional areas as needed

COMMAND STAFF

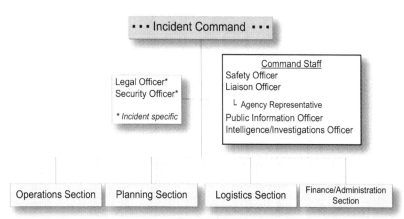

"The Command Staff in relationship to Incident Commander and General Staff"

Public Information Officer (PIO)

The PIO is responsible for developing and releasing information about the incident to the news media, to incident personnel, and to other appropriate agencies and organizations.

Only one primary PIO will be assigned for each incident, including incidents operating under a Unified Command and multi-jurisdiction incidents. The PIO may have assistants as necessary, and the assistants may also represent assisting agencies or jurisdictions.

Agencies have different policies and procedures for handling public information. The following are the major responsibilities of the PIO, which would generally apply on any incident.

The major responsibilities of the PIO are:

a. Review Common Responsibilities in Chapter 2

b. Determine from the IC/UC if there are any limitations on information release

c. Develop material for use in media briefings

d. Obtain IC approval of media releases

e. Inform media and conduct media briefings

f. Arrange for tours and other interviews or briefings that may be required

g. Manage a Joint Information Center (JIC) if established

h. Obtain media information that may be useful to incident planning

i. Maintain current information summaries and/or displays on the incident and provide information on the status of the incident to assigned personnel

j. Keep IC/UC briefed on PIO issues and concerns

k. Ensure that all required agency forms, reports and documents are completed prior to demobilization

l. Have debriefing session with the IC prior to demobilization

m. Maintain Unit Log (ICS-214)

Liaison Officer (LOFR)

Incidents that are multi-jurisdictional, or that have several agencies involved, may require the establishment of the LOFR position on the Command Staff. Only one primary LOFR will be assigned for each incident, including incidents operating under a UC and multi-jurisdiction incidents.

The LOFR may have assistants as necessary, and the assistants may also represent assisting agencies or jurisdictions. The LOFR is assigned to the incident to be the contact for assisting and/or cooperating Agency Representatives.

The major responsibilities of the LOFR are:

    a. Review Common Responsibilities in Chapter 2

    b. Be a contact point for Agency Representatives

    c. Maintain a list of assisting and cooperating agencies and Agency Representatives, including name and contact information. Monitor check-in sheets daily to ensure that all Agency Representatives are identified

    d. Assist in establishing and coordinating interagency contacts

    e. Keep agencies supporting the incident aware of the incident status

    f. Monitor incident operations to identify current or potential inter-organizational problems

    g. Participate in planning meetings, providing limitations and capabilities of assisting agency resources

    h. Coordinate response resource needs for incident investigation activities with the OSC

i.   Coordinate activities of visiting dignitaries

j.   Keep IC/UC briefed on agency issues and concerns

k.   Ensure that all required agency forms, reports and documents are completed prior to demobilization

l.   Have debriefing session with the IC prior to demobilization

m. Maintain Unit Log (ICS-214)

Agency Representative (AREP)

In many multi-jurisdiction incidents, an agency or jurisdiction may send an AREP who is not on direct tactical assignment, but is there to assist in coordination efforts.

An AREP is an individual assigned to an incident from an assisting or cooperating agency who has been delegated authority to make decisions on matters affecting that agency's participation at the incident. AREPs report to the LOFR or to the IC in the absence of a LOFR.

The major responsibilities of the AREPs are:

a. Review Common Responsibilities in Chapter 2

b. Ensure that all agency resources are properly checked in to the incident

c. Obtain a briefing from the LOFR or IC

d. Inform assisting or cooperating agency personnel on the incident that the AREP position for that agency has been filled

e. Attend briefings and planning meetings as required

f. Provide input on the use of agency resources unless resource Technical Specialists (THSP) are assigned from the agency

g. Cooperate fully with the IC/UC and the General Staff on agency involvement at the incident

h. Ensure the well-being of agency personnel assigned to the incident

i. Advise the LOFR of any special agency needs or requirements

j. Report to home agency dispatch or headquarters on a pre-arranged schedule

k. Ensure that all agency personnel and equipment are properly accounted for and released prior to departure

l. Ensure that all required agency forms, reports and documents are completed prior to demobilization

m. Have a debriefing session with the LOFR or IC before demobilization

n. Maintain Unit Log (ICS-214)

Safety Officer (SOF)

The SOF function is to develop and recommend measures for assuring personnel safety and to assess and/or anticipate hazardous and unsafe situations. Only one primary SOF will be assigned for each incident.

The SOF may have assistants, as necessary, and the assistants may also represent assisting agencies or jurisdictions. Safety assistants may have specific responsibilities, such as air operations, hazardous materials, etc.

The major responsibilities of the SOF are:

a. Review Common Responsibilities in Chapter 2

b. Participate in tactics and planning meetings, and other meetings and briefings as required

c. Identify hazardous situations associated with the incident

d. Review the IAP for safety implications

e. Provide safety advice in the IAP

f. Exercise emergency authority to stop and prevent unsafe acts

g. Investigate accidents that have occurred within the incident area

h. Assign assistants, as needed

i. Review and approve the Medical Plan (ICS-206)

j. Develop the Site Safety Plan

k. Keep IC/UC briefed on safety issues and concerns

l. Ensure that all required agency forms, reports and documents are completed prior to demobilization

m. Have debriefing session with the IC prior to demobilization

n. Maintain Unit Log (ICS-214)

Intelligence Officer (INTO)

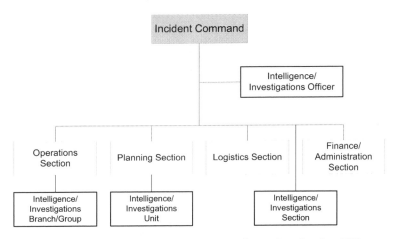

"The Intelligence/Investigations function in the ICS organization"

The intelligence/investigations function can be located at several levels within the ICS organization: as an Intelligence/Investigations Officer, Intelligence/Investigations Section Chief, Intelligence/Investigations Branch or Group in Operations, or as an Intelligence/Investigations Unit in Planning.

The role of the intelligence/investigations function in an ICS organization is to provide support to the IC/UC by establishing a system for the collection, analysis, and sharing of information developed during intelligence and investigations efforts.

The major responsibilities of the INTO are:

a. Review Common Responsibilities in Chapter 2

b. Participate in meetings and briefings as required

c. Collect and analyze incoming intelligence information from all sources

d. Determine the applicability, significance, and reliability of incoming intelligence information

e. Provide intelligence briefings to the IC/UC

f. Provide intelligence briefings in support of the ICS Planning Cycle

g. Provide Situation Unit with periodic updates of intelligence issues that impact the incident response

h. Review the IAP for intelligence implications

i. Answer intelligence questions and advise Command and General Staff as appropriate

j. Supervise, coordinate, and participate in the collection, analysis, processing, and dissemination of intelligence

k. Assist in establishing and maintaining systematic, cross-referenced intelligence records and files

l. Establish liaison with all participating law enforcement agencies

m. Conduct first order analysis on all incoming intelligence and fuse all applicable incoming intelligence with current intelligence holdings in preparation for briefings

n. Prepare all required intelligence reports and plans

o. As the incident dictates, determine need for Intelligence Technical Specialists in the Planning and Operations Sections

p. Ensure that all required agency forms, reports and documents are completed prior to demobilization

q. Conduct debriefing with the IC prior to demobilization

r. Maintain Unit Log (ICS-214)

Guidance to Help Determine Where to Locate the Intelligence/Investigations Function

Where to locate the intelligence/investigations function within the organization will be determined by the Incident Commander/Unified Command based on the incident or event. To help the IC/UC decide where to place the intelligence/investigations function in the ICS organization the guidance below may be helpful:

Intelligence/Investigations Officer

For incidents that require little need for tactical or classified intelligence or ongoing investigative activities.

Intelligence/Investigations Unit within the Planning Section

For incidents that require some degree of tactical/classified intelligence and/or limited investigative activities, but where an intelligence/investigations representative is not a member of the Unified Command.

Branch Director in the Operations Section

For incidents where there's a high degree of linkage and coordination between the tactical operations and the intelligence/investigations function.

Intelligence/Investigations Section Chief

For those incidents that are heavily influenced by intelligence/investigations or when multiple intelligence and/or investigative agencies are involved, a separate section may be necessary. Especially when there is highly technical or specialized intelligence/ investigative information that requires analysis. A terrorist incident would most likely require this level of intelligence/investigation organization within the Incident Management Team.

<u>Other Functions that you may see at the Command Staff Level</u>

The complexity of some all-hazard responses, may require the Incident Commander/Unified Command (IC/UC) to assign additional Command Staff positions to help support the incident response. A terrorist caused incident is a good example of where the IC/UC might find it critically important to expand beyond the traditional Command Staff functions.

Two Command Staff positions that an IC/UC may add to their team are a Legal Officer and a Security Officer. The need for the IC/UC to have ready access to the expertise and advice of a legal and security professional will dictate whether to add those functions to the Command Staff.

Ideally, the IC/UC will make the determination to add these positions early on in the response. If span-of-control becomes an issue, the IC/UC can assign a deputy to oversee all of the Command Staff functions.

Legal Officer

The major responsibilities of the Legal Officer are:

a. Review Common responsibilities in Chapter 2

b. Obtain a briefing from the IC/UC

c. Discuss with IC/UC expectations

d. Determine level of legal staffing required to support the incident

e. Work with Logistics to establish work area for legal staff

f. Assign task and supervise staff

g. Attend required meetings and briefings and be prepared to discuss legal issues impacting the response

h. Review and document Command's legal decisions and directives

i. Review authorities and legislative directives

j. Ensure documentation process meets agency/organizational requirements

k. Provide legal advice to Command and other IMT staff

l. Facilitate congressional inquires

m. Review agreements and interagency contracts

n. Help to resolve any labor issues

o. Respond to ethic issues

p. Work with the Liaison Officer to help resolve any legal interagency issues or concerns

q. Review all plans to ensure compliance with legislative mandates

r. Work with the Finance Section to help resolve contractor disputes

s. Ensure that Command is following agency/organization policy and guidelines

t. Maintain Unit Log (ICS-214)

Security Officer

The major responsibilities of the Security Officer are:

a. Review Common responsibilities in Chapter 2

b. Obtain a briefing from the IC/UC

c. Discuss with IC/UC expectations

d. Determine level of security staffing required to support the incident

e. Work with Logistics to establish work area for security staff

f. Assign task and supervise staff

g. Attend required meetings and briefings and be prepared to provide input on any security issues

h. Develop and monitor implementation of the Incident Security Plan

i. Evaluate planned action to determine potential security breach issues

j. Brief all in-coming IMT team members on badging and facility security protocols

k. Ensure that VIP security and site visit clearances are in place

l. Ensure that incident documentation security is established and followed

m. Work with security advance teams to ensure that requirements for visiting dignitaries are in place

n. Ensure that appropriate personnel security clearances are in place and monitored

o. Ensure that secure communications and meeting rooms are adequate

p. If needed, work with Operations on force protection requirements for field responders

q. Ensure that Community Outreach Teams are properly briefed on security issues for their assigned areas

r. Coordinate with state and local law enforcement officials on security issues

s. Ensure close coordination with Logistics Section on incident support facility security

t. Constantly evaluate negative public perception for potential down range security impacts

u. Maintain Unit Log (ICS-214)

COMMAND STAFF GUIDES

This Chapter is designed to help you if you are serving as a Public Information Officer, Liaison Officer, or Safety Officer.

———————————

✓ *PIO Pre-incident Planning*

✓ *PIO Briefing Checklist*

✓ *Initial Actions of the PIO*

✓ *Documenting the PIO Effort*

✓ *Risk Communications*

✓ *PIO Role in the ICS Planning Process*

✓ *Liaison Officer*

✓ *Some Best Practices for Managing the Stakeholders*

✓ *LOFR Role in the ICS Planning Process*

✓ *Safety Officer Briefing Checklist*

✓ *SOF Staffing Guide*

✓ *SOF Role in the ICS Planning Process*

———————————

Public Information Officer Pre-Incident Planning

If you know ahead of time that you can potentially be involved in an incident as your agency's PIO, there are a number of actions you can take to prepare well before an incident occurs. Below are some of those actions:

- ☐ *Have existing contacts with the media outlets in your area*

- ☐ *Know who all of your counterparts (fellow PIOs) are before an incident occurs*

- ☐ *Maintain up-to-date contact lists for all forms of media*

- ☐ *Understand your agency's policies regarding release of incident information*

- ☐ *Establish a process for the release of incident information that enables rapid dissemination of that information (e.g., press releases, updates)*

- ☐ *Establish processes in advance to support the assessment of public perceptions during an incident*

Public Information Officer Briefing Checklist

At a minimum the briefing should include:

- *Incident situation: magnitude and potential of the incident*
- *Political, environmental, and economic constraints*
- *Communities impacted*
- *Facilities already established (e.g., Joint Information Center)*
- *Stakeholders*
- *Level of media interest*
- *Any scheduled press briefings*
- *Gather basic facts about the incident*
    - *Who is involved in incident and response*
    - *What is the nature of the incident*
    - *When did the incident occur*
    - *Where did the incident occur*
    - *How did the incident occur (if known and releasable)*
- *Priorities and objectives*
- *Command structure (single or unified)*
- *Operational period*
- *Information on committed resources*
- *Incident investigation*
- *Incident organization*
- *Meeting schedule, if established*

Initial Actions of the PIO

During the early phases of a response, the actions taken by the PIO may have a significant impact not only on the success of this position, but on the positive perception of the overall response. Below are some of the initial-response actions that you, as the PIO, will need to consider:

- *Establish a dedicated phone line(s) for inquiries from the media*

- *Familiarize yourself with Unified Command members*

- *Write initial news release and get approval from the Incident Commander/Unified Command prior to actual release*

- *Fax and/or e-mail information release to media distribution list*

- *Recommend to the IC/UC a location for the JIC near the Incident Command Post*

- *Assign and staff positions in the JIC for data gathering and dissemination*

- *Develop talking points and command messages for the incident (e.g., what message does the IC/UC want to get across to the public)*

- *Coordinate a press conference with Unified Command to brief the media and public about the incident*

- *Develop an opening statement for Incident Commander/Unified Command prior to press conferences*

- *Create press packages*

Documenting the Public Information Effort

It's important to document your actions on the incident. Work closely with the Documentation Unit Leader to ensure that you are capturing the right information. At a minimum maintain the following records:

- Media calls
- Press releases
- Press packages
- Communications plans
- Questions and Answers or Frequently Asked Questions with answers developed for the incident
- Talking points
- Speaker preparations
- Fact sheets
- Video news clips
- Paper news clips
- Unit Log, ICS-214
- Develop outreach materials for the public (e.g., claims brochures, help numbers) and the responders (e.g., phone lists, media protocols)

Risk Communication

Risk communication is maximizing public safety by presenting information to the public in a timely and professional manner during emergency situations. Maximum cooperation is needed from the public to ensure safe response efforts. In today's environment, Incident Commanders have the responsibility to communicate risks to the public concerned with terrorism, homeland security, environmental disasters, and other incidents and events of public concern. A few examples of incidents that will involve risk communications:

- Natural disasters (e.g., hurricanes)
- Disease outbreaks (e.g., avian flu)
- Hazardous material releases
- Major bridge or building collapses
- Urban/wildland interface fires
- Terrorist attacks

Good Guidance when Communicating Risk

- Define all technical terms and acronyms – Don't speak in a manner that your audience will not understand

- Use positive or neutral terms – Don't refer to other disasters (e.g., Northridge Earthquake)

- Use visual aids to emphasize key points – Don't rely entirely on words

- Remain calm and use questions or allegations to say something positive – Don't let personal feelings interfere with your ability to communicate properly

- Use examples, stories, and analogies to establish a common understanding

- Be sensitive to nonverbal messages that you're communicating – Don't allow your message to be inconsistent with your position in the room, your dress, or your body language

- Emphasize achievements made and ongoing efforts – Don't guarantee anything

- Provide information on what is being done – Don't speculate about worst cases

- Use personal pronouns – Don't identify yourself as the entire organization

Communicating Risk During the Initial Phase of an Incident

- Work with the Liaison Officer to identify stakeholders:
    - Impacted private sector entities
    - Public
    - Regulatory agencies
    - Specific population segments (e.g., old, young, certain geographic area, etc.)
    - Other agencies specifically involved in an incident/event
- Get the word out in emergency situations through widespread distribution of material to ensure effective communication (e.g., press releases, press conferences, television and radio, and public meetings and new media)
- During an initial response, the first responders may need to brief the public on inherent safety concerns. Prepare, review, remain calm, and know your audience

Communicating Risk during the Project Phase of the Response

- Working with the stakeholders and the Liaison Officer, develop a plan of action to organize and disseminate information to the public
- Use the following checklist to prepare for a speaking engagement

Checklist to Prepare for Speaking Engagements

- ☐ *Time, place, and date of public appearance*

- ☐ *Incident/event name: time, place, and date of incident/ event*

- ☐ *Introduction: statement of personal concern, statement of organization commitment, and the purpose and plan for the meeting*

- ☐ *Key messages: supporting data of the incident specifically impacting the public*

- ☐ *Public involvement: names and concerns of who are helping, the organizations they represent, and their specific area of responsibility (if a volunteer group has been established, now is a good time to mention how the community can get involved). Let the public know what they can do to help (whether that is evacuating, staying indoors, or reporting suspicious activity)*

- ☐ *Conclusion: summary statement*

- ☐ *Questions and answers: practice anticipated questions and responses*

- ☐ *Presentation material: handouts, audios, etc.*

Public Information Officer's Role in the ICS Planning Process

Command and General Staff Meeting

As the PIO, your role in the Command and General Staff Meeting is to listen to the priorities, limitations and constraints, and response objectives, and clearly understand the intent and focus of the IC/UC in order to effectively communicate that to the public and to the other responding agencies.

As the response matures, you may also use this meeting to discuss how the response is being perceived by the public and any potential actions that the IC/UC may need to take to correct any misconceptions and maintain/reinforce the positive perceptions.

This meeting is designed so that the IC/UC and their staff can discuss issues. Below are a few examples of what you might want to discuss at the meeting:

- Get clarification on the media strategy and command's focus
- Agree on press interviews and timelines
- Agree on how to manage sensitive information
- Identify the location and interagency staffing of the Joint Information Center
- Report out to the IC/UC on media perception of the response

Planning Meeting

You should use this meeting to learn what the intended strategies and tactics are for the upcoming operational period. This meeting gives the PIO an operational snapshot of what is planned and can assist in determining the types of media communications that will be necessary to support the ongoing operations.

This meeting may also be used to determine the appropriate time when a press availability or tour of the operational sites might be appropriate. You'll also have an opportunity to cover any issues with respect to responder interactions with the media and public perceptions of the response.

Operations Briefing

The Operations Briefing is where the Operations Section Chief will brief incoming Branch Directors, Division and Group Supervisors, and Staging Area Managers. There will be an opportunity for you to say a few words. Some areas that you may want to cover are:

- Any media interaction opportunities with oncoming shift supervisors

- The "dos" and "don'ts" of talking with the media

- JIC contact phone numbers

Liaison Officer

Once you arrive on scene, you'll need to quickly establish yourself as a point of contact for Agency Representatives and stakeholders. Before you do that, make sure that you check in to the incident and get a briefing from the Incident Commander or a representative of the Unified Command.

Use the checklist below as a memory jogger for the questions that you would like answered.

- ☐ Incident situation: magnitude and potential of the incident
- ☐ Information on any current liaison activities
- ☐ Names of assisting and cooperating agencies
- ☐ Names of any concerned stakeholders
- ☐ Incident priorities, limitations, constraints, and objectives
- ☐ Current incident organizational structure
- ☐ Expected incident duration
- ☐ Estimate on the potential size of the response organization
- ☐ Initial instructions concerning the tasks expected of the Liaison Officer
- ☐ Operational Period
- ☐ Agencies and jurisdictions involved

Some Best Practices for Managing the Stakeholders

Experienced Liaison Officers have learned some hard lessons as they have carried out their duties. Below are a few tips that may help you avoid learning the same lessons, the hard way.

Elected Officials and their staff

- Ensure that elected officials are briefed prior to a significant press release or media event
- Be aware of who will be making the formal inquiries, who the key staff members are, and what specific concerns or "hot topics" they have
- Determine the need to develop a detailed agenda and briefing packages for VIP visitors
- Work with the affected State Incident Commander to identify the appropriate escort for any VIP visits
- Try and group political/VIP visits together

Government agencies

- Be cognizant of which government agencies have reported in to the response and which have not
- Initiate contact with those agencies not represented
- Offer to provide periodic situational updates, informal consultations, or requests for support as the response develops

General public

- Combine your efforts with the Public Information Officer (PIO) and his/her staff
- Use targeted press releases generated by the PIO
- Consider community outreach through community meetings
- Use local elected officials to help organize outreach events

Industry partners

- Use the response as an opportunity to reinforce key relationships

Liaison Officer's Role in the ICS Planning Process

Two of the more important meetings that you will be attending are the Command and General Staff Meeting and the Planning Meeting.

Command and General Staff Meeting

The information discussed during this meeting will set into motion the development of an Incident Action Plan. The IC/UC will lay out the objectives for the next operational period, set the priorities, discuss issues of concern, assign tasking to individual command team members, and discuss how they see the response progressing. You need to take good notes because you'll be dealing with agency representatives and stakeholders such as elected officials and you must be intimately familiar with all aspects of the response.

This meeting is meant to be a two-way discussion, so take a few minutes to let the IC/UC know of problems you foresee and potential solutions. As Liaison Officer, you may become aware of concerns expressed by the elected officials, community stakeholders, or other organizations. If you cannot address an issue, you'll need to bring it to the IC/UC for resolution.

Planning Meeting

The Planning Meeting is another good opportunity to gain current information on the incident so that you have the most recent situational update and future direction. Some issues that you may want to comment on if they are applicable:

- Emerging concerns from elected officials or stakeholders
- Cooperating and Assisting Agency limitations or resource constraints
- Conflicts involving agency or organization jurisdictions, policies or procedures that may affect response management efficiency
- Requested visits by dignitaries or elected officials
- Reports on dignitary visits, expressed reactions, and anticipated follow-up actions

Safety Officer Briefing Checklist

This checklist can help remind you of questions you would like answered before assuming responsibility for the safety function for the incident.

- *Incident situation: magnitude and potential of the incident*
- *Information on any current safety activities*
- *Results of any risk assessments*
- *Incident priorities, limitations, and constraints*
- *Incident objectives*
- *Current incident organizational structure*
- *Expected incident duration*
- *Estimate on the potential size of the response organization*
- *Operational Period*
- *Agencies and jurisdictions involved*
- *Review of any accidents, injuries, or near misses*
- *Clarify your authority to stop work*

Safety Officer Staffing Guide

You want to take a hard look at the safety issues you're facing to determine the level of support you'll require. Below are some guidelines that you can use to help you determine the number of Assistant Safety Officers you may require:

- One Assistant Safety Officer for each high-risk activity
- One Assistant Safety Officer for every 100 responders
- One Assistant Safety Officer for completing the Site Safety Plan and providing input into the Incident Action Plan
- One Assistant Safety Officer to coordinate air monitoring or other specialized assessments
- One Assistant Safety Officer available to assist the Operations Section Chief with real-time tactical decisions
- One Assistant Safety Officer to support multiple incident support facilities

Safety Officer's Role in the ICS Planning Process

Command and General Staff Meeting

This meeting is an excellent forum for you to ask for clarification on any issues with which you are uncomfortable and to discuss any safety concerns. Make sure you are aware of your authority, and, if possible, try to ensure that one of the incident objectives is focused on safety. For example - Ensure that all operations are conducted in accordance with safe work practices.

Tactics Meeting

Your responsibility as the Safety Officer in this meeting is very clear: help the Operations Section Chief create a safe plan to achieve the IC/UC objectives. This meeting is totally focused on the development of the Operations Section Chief's tactical plan for the next operational period.

As the Safety Officer, you're evaluating the risks and benefits of the various strategies and tactics that the OSC would like to use to accomplish the objectives for which he or she is responsible.

If you determine that a specific strategy or tactic presents an unacceptable risk to the responders, then you have the opportunity to take the concern up with the OSC and the PSC. This should be a discussion that communicates the perceived risks and mitigations that may be incorporated to protect responders. Some specific responsibilities that you have at the Tactics Meeting include:

- Conducting a hazard/risk analysis
- Providing mitigation recommendations to control hazards (e.g., personal protective equipment, air monitoring)
- Evaluating the need to embed Assistant Safety Officers in Operations to monitor hazardous evolutions

Using the ICS-215, Operational Planning Worksheet

The Tactics Meeting works with the Operations Section Chief using an ICS-215 Operational Planning Worksheet to develop a tactical plan. The worksheet is designed to walk the OSC through the development of the plan. As the Safety Officer, you'll be providing input as the plan is laid out.

In the example ICS-215, you'll see where the OSC has created a Search Group as part of their organization. Next to the Search Group, the OSC has developed a work assignment that the Search Group is to accomplish (Block 5).

Pay particular attention to this block. Evaluate the work assignment from a safety perspective and let the OSC know if you see any potential safety problems and have any recommendations for mitigating actions.

OPERATIONAL PLANNING WORKSHEET

1. INCIDENT NAME MERIDIAN FLOOD

6. KIND OF RESOURCES

4. DIVISION/ GROUP/ OTHER LOCATION	5. WORK ASSIGNMENTS	Ambulance (type 2)	Helicopter
Search Group	Conduct house-to-house search for injured persons. Mark each dwelling searched with a red "X" on the front door. Evacuate injured persons to triage center.	REQ	
		HAVE	
		NEED	

"The upper left side of the ICS-215, Operational Planning Worksheet"

Upper Right Corner of the Operational Planning Worksheet

On the right side of the ICS-215, the OSC accounts for the number of supervisors needed to manage the tactical operations. In addition, the OSC will list specialized skills that he or she needs to support the Search Group's operations. You can see that an Assistant Safety Officer has been listed specifically to support the Search Group.

The designation of an Assistant Safety Officer to serve in the Search Group came about either because the OSC is aware of the inherent risk of the work assignment the Search Group performs, or you, the Safety Officer, have recommended to the OSC to consider an Assistant Safety Officer because of the safety implications.

The ICS-215 will cover every tactical operation planned for the next operational period.

2. DATE & TIME PREPARED		3. OPERATIONAL PERIOD (DATE & TIME)	
15 Nov 2100		16 Nov 0600 to 16 Nov 1800	
7. OVERHEAD	8. SPECIAL EQUIPMENT & SUPPLIES	9. REPORTING LOCATION	10. REQUESTED ARRIVAL TIME
Supervisor Assistant Safety Officer	Red Spray Paint	4th Street and County Road 502	0530
Rescue Boat			
1			
Search Team (six person)			
1			

"Upper right side of the ICS-215, Operational Planning Worksheet"

Planning Meeting

As the Safety Officer, your input is critical. When high-risk activities are going to be conducted you need to reassure the Command that you and the OSC have worked out mitigating controls to protect the responders.

For example, when overhauling a large manufacturing facility following an intense fire the firefighters are at risk from falling debris and collapsing structures.

Mitigation efforts might include pre-assessments by engineers before the firefighters enter the structure as well as the use of a "buddy system" and a rescue team with a crane.

As the Safety Officer, you have to ensure that the IC/UC understand the risks and the mitigations. You want to come to the meeting prepared to discuss:

- Incident hazard/risk analysis and identified mitigating factors
- The Site Safety Plan
- Your commitment to and support of the Incident Action Plan

Safety Officer's Role in the Development of the ICS-204, Assignment List

ICS-204 Assignment Lists provide the work assignments for Branches, Divisions, Groups, and Staging Areas. You need to review every ICS-204. There's space on the form to put down specific safety instructions that are tailored to the work that a particular Division or Group will be performing.

Some examples of special instructions might include:

- An Assistant Safety Officer must be present at all times that this activity is being conducted

- Work in teams of two or more at all times

- Snakes are suspected to be in the work area, wear snake gators and carry snakebite kits

- A half-face respirator with organic vapor cartridges is required for work when workers are within 100 feet of the pipeline rupture area. Air monitoring will be conducted by the assigned Assistant Safety Officer. Only approved workers are authorized to work in areas requiring respiratory protection

- Flammable vapors are present in the work area. All equipment and communications devices must be explosion proof, spark resistant, or intrinsically safe

Example ICS-204

1. BRANCH	2. ~~DIVISION~~/GROUP Search	ASSIGNMENT LIST

3. INCIDENT NAME **MERIDIAN FLOOD**	4. OPERATIONAL PERIOD (Date and Time) 16 Nov 0600 to 16 Nov 1800

5. OPERATIONS PERSONNEL

OPERATIONS CHIEF _____ L. Hewett _____ ~~DIVISION~~/GROUP SUPERVISOR _____ P. Robert _____

BRANCH DIRECTOR _____ AIR TACTICAL GROUP SUPERVISOR _____

6. RESOURCES ASSIGNED THIS PERIOD

STRIKE TEAM/TASK FORCE RESOURCE DESIGNATOR	EMT	LEADER	NUMBER PERSONS	TRANS NEEDED	DROP OFF POINT/TIME	PICK UP POINT/TIME
MESA #3		B. Riggs	21		0530	
44120		V. Kammer	4		0530	
Ambulance #1		S. Miller	2		0530	
Helicopter 12		T. Troutman	2			

7. ASSIGNMENT

Conduct house-to-house search for injured persons. Mark each dwelling searched with a red "X" on the front door. Evacuate injured persons to triage center.

8. SPECIAL INSTRUCTIONS

Work in teams of two or more at all times. Snakes are suspected to be in the work area, wear snake gators. Personal floatation devices should be worn. Daylight operations only. Conduct regular communications checks. Send hourly updates on the group's progress to the Situation Unit.

9. DIVISION/GROUP COMMUNICATIONS SUMMARY

FUNCTION		FREQ.	SYSTEM	CHAN.	FUNCTION		FREQ.	SYSTEM	CHAN.
COMMAND	LOCAL	CDF 1	King	1	SUPPORT	LOCAL			
	REPEAT					REPEAT			
DIV./GROUP TACTICAL		157.4505	King	3	GROUND TO AIR				

PREPARED BY (RESOURCES UNIT LEADER) A. Worth	APPROVED BY (PLANNING SECT. CH.) J. Gafkjen	DATE 16 Nov	TIME 0400

"ICS-204 — Assignment List"

Operations Briefing

The Operations Section Chief will brief his or her personnel to ensure that each one understands what is expected of them. You'll have an opportunity to say a few words on safety. Your primary message should be to emphasize the hazards that the field responders are facing and the importance of following the hazard mitigation strategies that have been put in place to ensure responder safety.

This might include a detailed discussion of the chemical hazards associated with styrene inhalation, a discussion of personal protective equipment, or emergency procedures for medical casualties or whatever is applicable.

Execute Plan and Assess Progress

Once the responders roll into the field and begin to implement the plan, you want to have your Assistant Safety Officers or yourself out there ensuring that work assignments are being conducted with responder safety as the priority. Those same assistants should be constantly assessing the risk.

This is especially critical in a very dynamic response or one where the complete situation on the ground is unknown. Work closely with the Division/Group Supervisors to better understand what they are up against.

OPERATIONS SECTION

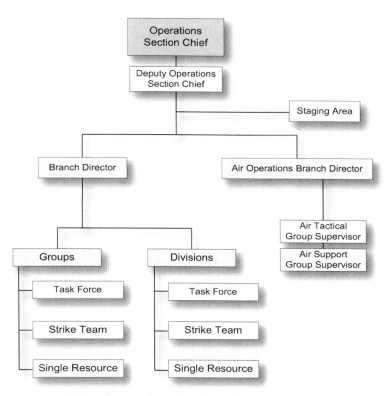

"The Operations Section Organization"

Operations Section Chief (OSC)

The OSC, a member of the General Staff, is responsible for the management of all tactical operations. The OSC will normally be selected from the organization/agency with the most jurisdictional responsibility for the incident.

The OSC activates and supervises organizational elements in accordance with the Incident Action Plan and directs its execution. The OSC also directs the preparation of operational plans; requests or releases resources; monitors operational progress and makes changes to the IAP as necessary; and reports such to the IC.

The OSC may have deputies, who may be from the same agency or from an assisting agency. The Deputy OSC must have the same qualifications as the person for whom he/she works, and must be ready to take over that position at any time.

In complex incidents, the OSC may assign a Deputy OSC to supervise on-scene operations while the OSC participates in the incident planning process.

The major responsibilities of the OSC are:

  a. Review Common Responsibilities in Chapter 2

  b. Obtain briefing from IC

  c. Evaluate and request sufficient Section supervisory staffing for both operational and planning activities

  d. Supervise Operations Section field personnel

  e. Implement the IAP for the Operations Section

f. Evaluate on-scene operations and make adjustments to organization, strategies, tactics, and resources as necessary

g. Ensure the Resources Unit is advised of changes in the status of resources assigned to the section

h. Ensure that Operations Section personnel execute work assignments following approved safe work practices

i. Monitor need for and request additional resources to support operations as necessary

j. Assemble/disassemble task forces/strike teams as appropriate

k. Identify staging areas

l. Evaluate and monitor current situation in preparing for the next operational period

m. Convert operational incident objectives into strategic and tactical options

n. Coordinate and consult with the PSC, Safety Officer, and technical specialists on selection of appropriate strategies and tactics to accomplish objectives

o. Identify kind, type and number of resources required to support selected strategies

p. Subdivide work areas into manageable units

q. Develop work assignments and allocate tactical resources based on strategic requirements using the ICS-215, Operational Planning Worksheet

r. Coordinate planned activities with the Safety Officer to ensure compliance with safety practices

s. Participate in the planning process and the development of the tactical portions of the IAP (ICS-204 and ICS-220)

t. Assist with development of long-range strategic, contingency, and demobilization plans

u. Develop recommended list of Section resources to be demobilized and initiate recommendation for release when appropriate

v. Receive and implement applicable portions of the incident Demobilization Plan

w. Participate in operational briefings to IMT members as well as briefings to media, and visiting dignitaries

x. Maintain Unit Log (ICS-214)

Branch Director (OPBD)

The Branch Directors when activated, are under the direction of the OSC and are responsible for the implementation of the portion of the IAP assigned to the Branch.

The major responsibilities of the OPBD are:

a. Review Common Responsibilities in Chapter 2

b. Receive briefing from the OSC and/or the person you're relieving

c. Identify Divisions, Groups, and resources assigned to the Branch

d. Ensure that Division and/or Group Supervisors (DIVS) have a copy of the IAP

e. Implement IAP for the Branch

f. Develop with subordinates alternatives for Branch control operations

g. Review Division/Group Assignment Lists (ICS-204) for Divisions/Groups within the Branch. Modify ICS-204 based on effectiveness of current operations

h. Assign specific work tasks to DIVS

i. Supervise Branch operations

j. Resolve logistic problems reported by subordinates

k. Attend planning meetings as requested by the OSC

l. Ensure, through chain of command, that the Resources Unit is advised of changes in the status of resources assigned to the Branch

m. Report to OSC when: the IAP is to be modified; additional resources are needed; surplus resources are available; or hazardous situations or significant events occur

n. Approve accident and medical reports (home agency forms) originating within the Branch

o. Consider demobilization of resources well in advance

p. Debrief with OSC and/or as directed at the end of each shift

q. Maintain Unit Log (ICS-214)

Division/Group Supervisor (DIVS)

The DIVS reports to the OSC (or OPBD when activated). The DIVS is responsible for the implementation of his/her assigned portion of the IAP, assignment of resources within the Division/Group, and reporting on the progress of operations and status of resources within the Division/Group.

The major responsibilities of the DIVS are:

a. Review Common Responsibilities in Chapter 2

b. Receive briefing from the OSC , OPBD and/or the person you're relieving

c. Identify resources assigned to the Division/ Group

d. Provide the IAP to subordinates, as needed

e. Review Division/Group assigned tasks, incident activities, and safety concerns with subordinates

f. Implement IAP for Division/Group

g. Supervise Division/Group resources and make changes as appropriate

h. Ensure, through chain of command, that Resources Unit is advised of all changes in the status of resources assigned to the Division/ Group

i. Coordinate activities with adjacent Division/ Group

j. Determine need for assistance on assigned tasks

k. Submit situation and resources status information to the Branch Director or the OSC as directed

l. Report hazardous situations, special occurrences, or significant events, (e.g., accidents, sickness, discovery of unanticipated sensitive resources, to the immediate supervisor)

m. Ensure that assigned personnel and equipment get to and from assignments in a timely and orderly manner

n. Resolve logistics problems within the Division/ Group

o. Participate in the development of Branch plans for the next operational period, as requested

p. Consider demobilization well in advance

q. Debrief as directed at the end of each shift

r. Maintain Unit Log (ICS-214)

Strike Team/Task Force Leader (STCR/TFLD)

The STCR/TFLD reports to an OPBD or DIVS and is responsible for performing specific tactical activities. The Leader reports work progress, resources status, and other important information and maintains work records on assigned personnel.

The major responsibilities of the STCR/TFLD are:

a. Review Common Responsibilities in Chapter 2

b. Receive briefing from the OSC, DIVS and/or the person you're relieving

c. Review assignments, safety concerns, and assign tasks with subordinates

d. Monitor work progress and make changes when necessary

e. Keep supervisor informed of progress and any changes

f. Coordinate activities with adjacent Strike Teams, Task Forces and single resources

g. Travel to and from active assignment area with assigned resources

h. Retain control of resources while in "assigned" or "out-of-service" status

i. Submit situation and resources status information through chain of command DIVS/OPBD/OSC as appropriate

j. Debrief as directed at the end of each shift

k. Maintain Unit Log (ICS-214)

Single Resource

A single resource is an individual, a piece of equipment and its personnel complement, or a crew or team of individuals with an identified work supervisor that can be used on an incident.

The major responsibilities of the person in charge of a single tactical resource are:

a. Review Common Responsibilities in Chapter 2

b. Review assignments

c. Receive briefing from the OSC, DIVS and/or the person you're relieving

d. Obtain necessary equipment and supplies

e. Review weather/environmental conditions for assignment area

f. Brief subordinates on safety measures

g. Monitor work progress

h. Ensure adequate communications with supervisor and subordinates

i. Keep supervisor informed of progress and any changes

j. Brief relief personnel, and advise them of any change in conditions

k. Return equipment and supplies to appropriate Logistic Unit

l. Complete and turn in all time and use records on personnel and equipment

m. Debrief as directed at the end of each shift

n. Maintain Unit Log (ICS-214)

Staging Area Manager (STAM)

The STAM is under the direction of the OSC and is responsible for managing all activities within a Staging Area.

The major responsibilities of the STAM are:

a. Review Common Responsibilities in Chapter 2

b. Receive briefing from the OSC, and/or the person you're relieving

c. Establish Staging Area layout

d. Determine any support needs for equipment, feeding, sanitation and security

e. Establish check-in function as appropriate

f. Ensure security of staged resources

g. Post areas for identification and traffic control

h. Request maintenance service for equipment at Staging Area as appropriate

i. Respond to requests for resource assignments (Note: This may be direct from the OSC or via the Incident Communications Center)

j. Obtain and issue receipts for radio equipment and other supplies distributed and received at Staging Area

k. Determine required resource levels that will be staged from the OSC

l. Advise the OSC when reserve levels reach minimums

m. Maintain and provide status to Resources Unit for all resources in Staging Area

n. Maintain Staging Area in orderly condition

o. Demobilize Staging Area in accordance with the Incident Action Plan

p. Debrief OSC as directed

q. Maintain Unit Log (ICS-214)

Air Operations Branch Director (AOBD)

The AOBD is ground-based and is primarily responsible for preparing the Air Operations Summary Worksheet (ICS-220), the air operations portion of the IAP and for providing logistical support to incident aircraft.

The Air Operations Summary Worksheet serves the same purpose as the Assignment List (ICS-204) does for other operational resources, by assigning and managing aviation resources on the incident.

The Air Operations Summary Worksheet may or may not be used, depending on the needs of the incident. After the IAP is approved, the AOBD is responsible for overseeing the tactical and logistical assignments of the Air Operations Branch. In coordination with the Logistics Section, the AOBD is responsible for providing logistical support to aircraft operating on the incident.

The major responsibilities of the AOBD are:

a. Review Common Responsibilities in Chapter 2

b. Organize air operations

c. Coordinate airspace use with the FAA. Request declaration (or cancellation) of Temporary Flight Restriction (TFR) IAW FAR 91.173 and post Notice to Airmen (NOTAM) as required

d. Attend the Tactics Meeting and Planning Meeting to obtain information for completing the Air Operations Summary Worksheet

e. Participate in preparation of the IAP through the OSC. Ensure that the air operations portion of the IAP takes into consideration the air traffic control requirements of assigned aircraft

f. Coordinate with the Communications Unit Leader (COML) to designate air tactical and support frequencies

g. Perform operational planning for air operations

h. Prepare and provide Air Operations Summary Worksheet to the Air Support Group and Fixed-Wing Bases

i. Supervise all air operations activities associated with the incident

j. Evaluate helibase and helispot locations

k. Establish procedures for emergency reassignment of aircraft

l. Coordinate approved flights of non-incident aircraft in the TFR(s)

m. Respond to requests for use of incident aircraft

n. Report to the OSC on air operations activities

o. Report special incidents/accidents

p. Develop Aviation Site Safety Plan in concert with Safety Officer

q. Arrange for an accident investigation team when warranted

r. Debrief with OSC as directed at the end of each shift

s. Maintain Unit Log (ICS-214)

Air Tactical Group Supervisor (ATGS)

The Air Tactical Group Supervisor is primarily responsible for the coordination of aircraft operations when fixed and/or rotary-wing aircraft are operating on an incident. The Air Tactical Group Supervisor performs these coordination activities while airborne. The Air Tactical Group Supervisor reports to the Air Operations Branch Director.

The major responsibilities of the ATGS are:

a. Review Common Responsibilities in Chapter 2

b. Obtain a copy of the IAP from the AOBD, including Air Operations Summary Worksheet (ICS-220), if completed

c. Participate in AOBD planning activities

d. Inform AOBD of group activities

e. Identify resources/supplies dispatched for the Air Tactical Group

f. Request special air tactical items from appropriate sources through Logistics Section

g. Coordinate activities with AOBD

h. Obtain assigned ground-to-air frequency for airbase operations from the Communications Unit Leader or Incident Radio Communications Plan (ICS-205)

i. Inform AOBD of capability to provide night flying service

j. Ensure compliance with each agency's operations checklist for day and night operations

k. Debrief as directed at the end of each shift

l. Maintain Unit Log (ICS-214)

Air Support Group Supervisor (ASGS)

The Air Support Group Supervisor is primarily responsible for supporting and managing Helibase and Helispot operations and maintaining liaison with fixed-wing air bases. This includes providing:

- Fuel and other supplies
- Maintenance and repair of helicopters
- Retardant mixing and loading
- Keeping records of helicopter activity
- Providing enforcement of safety regulations

These major functions are performed at Helibases and Helispots. Helicopters during landing and take-off and while on the ground are under the control of the Air Support Group's Helibase or Helispot Managers. The Air Support Group Supervisor reports to the Air Operations Branch Director.

The major responsibilities of the ASGS are:

a. Review Common Responsibilities in Chapter 2

b. Obtain a copy of the IAP from the AOBD, including Air Operations Summary Worksheet (ICS-220), if completed

c. Participate in AOBD planning activities

d. Inform AOBD of group activities

e. Identify resources/supplies dispatched for the Air Support Group

f. Request special air support items from appropriate sources through Logistics Section

g. Determine need for assignment of personnel and equipment at each airbase

h. Coordinate activities with AOBD

i. Obtain assigned ground-to-air frequency for airbase operations from the Communications Unit Leader or Incident Radio Communications Plan (ICS-205)

j. Inform AOBD of capability to provide night flying service

k. Ensure compliance with each agency's protocols for day and night operations

l. Ensure dust abatement procedures are implemented at helibases and helispots

m. Provide crash-rescue service for helibases and helispots

n. Debrief as directed at the end of each shift

o. Maintain Unit Log (ICS-214)

OPERATIONS SECTION CHIEF GUIDES

This Chapter is designed to help the Operations Section Chief (OSC) accomplish his or her responsibilities.

- ✓ *Operations Section Chief In-Brief Checklist*
- ✓ *Preparing for the Pre-Tactics Meeting*
- ✓ *OSC Responsibilities During the Tactics Meeting*
- ✓ *Tactics Meeting Preparation Guide*
- ✓ *Completing the ICS-215*
- ✓ *Supervisor Expectations*
- ✓ *Operations Section Chief and Deputy Operations Section Chief Duties*
- ✓ *OSC Responsibilities During the Planning Meeting*
- ✓ *OSC Responsibilities in Reviewing the ICS-204, Assignment List*
- ✓ *OSC Readiness Checklist for the Operations Briefing*
- ✓ *Operations Briefing Checklist*
- ✓ *Sample Operations Briefing*
- ✓ *Daily Self-Evaluation of the Operations Section*

<u>Operations Section Chief In-Brief Checklist</u>

As the OSC, you are going to have to come up to speed quickly on the incident situation, understand the response objectives and priorities, gain familiarity with the operations organization that you're inheriting, and what resources are committed to the response.

This knowledge can be achieved only by having a thorough briefing from the IC or the off-going Operations Section Chief. Use the checklist below to help guide you as you receive your briefing:

- ☐ *Incident situation: magnitude and potential of the incident*
- ☐ *Political, environmental, and economic constraints*
- ☐ *Facilities already established (including Staging Areas)*
- ☐ *Priorities and objectives*
- ☐ *Command structure (single or unified)*
- ☐ *Agencies and jurisdictions involved*
- ☐ *Information on committed resources*
- ☐ *Resources ordered*
- ☐ *Incident investigation*
- ☐ *Resource-request process*
- ☐ *Operations organization*
- ☐ *Support organization (Planning, Logistics, etc.)*
- ☐ *Communications schedule with supervisors and leaders*
- ☐ *Meeting schedule, if established*

Make sure you request a copy of the ICS-201, Incident Briefing Form, or if available, the Incident Action Plan. These documents will help you manage your responsibilities.

Once you have assumed the role of the OSC ask yourself the following questions:

- *Are operations being conducted safely?*
- *Is the current operations organization adequate for the situation on the ground?*
- *Is my span-of-control within acceptable limits?*
- *What can go wrong?*
- *Do the supervisors and leaders know that I am now the OSC?*

Preparing for the Pre-Tactics Meeting

Once you leave the Command and General Staff Meeting, you need to start working on your tactical plan. Using the objectives that the Incident Commander/ Unified Command set for the next operational period, identify which ones belong to Operations and start building your plan.

Do not leave your planning for the Tactics Meeting if the incident is large or complex, as you will not have enough time to thoroughly work through all of the steps involved in putting your tactical plan together prior to the Planning Meeting. Use the guides that follow to help you through your planning.

Operations Section Chief's Responsibilities During The Tactics Meeting

This meeting is totally focused on the development of the Operations Section Chief's tactical plan for the next operational period. As the OSC, you have a number of responsibilities during the meeting so we recommend you use the checklist below:

- ☐ *Review incident objectives and priorities and identify which objectives belong to Operations*

- ☐ *Analyze the overall situation and determine complexity of tasks to be conducted*

- ☐ *Develop overall management strategy (e.g., safety first, rescue and fire control second)*

- ☐ *Identify functions that have to be performed to implement strategies (search and rescue, security, etc.)*

- ☐ *Complete the Operational Planning Worksheet, ICS-215*

  - ☐ *Subdivide incident into manageable work units (groups, divisions, etc.)*

  - ☐ *Identify work assignments*

  - ☐ *Identify resource requirements to achieve each work assignment*

  - ☐ *Identify overhead staffing needs to support each work assignment (e.g., supervisor, Assistant Safety Officer)*

  - ☐ *Identify specialized equipment and supply needs for each work assignment (e.g., intrinsically safe radios)*

  - ☐ *Specify reporting times and locations for personnel*

- ☐ *Identify support facilities (e.g., Staging Areas, Helibases)*

- ☐ *Review contingencies*

- Develop an Operations Section organization chart, check span-of-control and match up with ICS-215 assignments

- Review planned actions against incident objectives and priorities (compare work assignments with the objectives to make sure every objective has been addressed)

10-5

Tactics Meeting Preparation Guide

For a tactics meeting to be successful, it is essential that the OSC follow five basic steps when developing the tactical plan for the next operations period.

First — review incident objectives and priorities and identify which objectives belong to Operations.

Second — analyze the overall situation and determine the complexity of the task at hand. Consult with Technical Specialist's as required.

Third — determine and document the overall strategy and tactics. This process will be used to implement the objectives and identify contingencies. The OSC may use a map/chart to help visualize possible strategies and tactics.

Fourth—identify functions (e.g., crowd control, fire fighting, mass casualty, booming, product recovery, assessment, law enforcement, air monitoring, search & rescue). This step must be taken prior to dividing the incident into manageable work units.

Fifth — subdivide the incident into manageable work units (divisions, groups, branches, etc, based on identified functions.) This information must be clearly displayed on a working map and a draft Operations Section Organization Chart as well as on the ICS-215.

Ensure the work units you identify are manageable and support the Incident Objectives. If the initial task of subdividing the incident is not done well, the consequences will be apparent.

Considerations when dividing an incident into manageable work assignments

There are several factors to take into consideration when dividing the incident into manageable work assignments (e.g., Branches, Divisions, Groups, Task Forces, Strike Teams). These include:

- Incident priorities
- Size of affected area
- Complexity of the incident and number of tasks to be performed
- Amount of work to be accomplished
- Span-of-control issues
- Water versus land
- Topography
- Logistics requirements
- Kind of functions to be accomplished
- Contingencies
- Limitations and constraints
- Safety issues
- Specific resource capabilities
- Training, experience, and availability of supervisory personnel
- Ability to communicate with resources

Final products from the tactics meeting should include:

- Working maps/charts/building plans
- Large (3'x5') ICS-215 Operational Planning Worksheet
- Small (8"x14") ICS-215 Operational Planning Worksheet
- Operations Section Organization Chart
- List of strategies that include any contingencies, or "what if" scenarios identified
- ICS-215A, Incident Action Plan Safety Analysis to be completed by the Safety Officer

Completing the ICS-215 Operational Planning Worksheet

Below is an example of the top left corner of the ICS-215. As the OSC, you list the organizational element (e.g., Search Group) in block 4; the work assignment in block 5; the kind and type of resources (e.g., Ambulance – type 2) in block 6; and, the number of resources that you require to do the assignment.

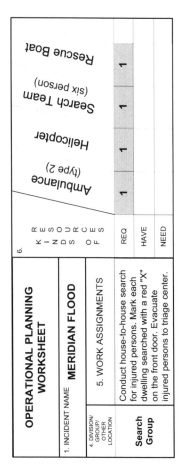

"ICS-215 Operational Planning Worksheet upper left corner"

Below is the upper right corner of the ICS-215. As the OSC, list any overhead personnel (e.g., Division Supervisor, Assistant Safety Officer) in block 7; special equipment (e.g., red spray paint) in block 8; reporting location in block 9; and, arrival time block 10.

	Rescue Boat	Search Team (six person)	Helicopter	Ambulance (type 2)
2. DATE & TIME PREPARED 15 Nov 2100				
7. OVERHEAD Supervisor	1			
Assistant Safety Officer		1		
8. SPECIAL EQUIPMENT & SUPPLIES Red Spray Paint			1	
3. OPERATIONAL PERIOD (DATE & TIME) 16 Nov 0600 to 16 Nov 1800				1
9. REPORTING LOCATION 4th Street and County Road 502				
10. REQUESTED ARRIVAL TIME 0530				

"ICS-215 Operational Planning Worksheet upper right corner"

Supervisor Expectations

There may be many supervisors working under you that come from other agencies so make sure that you convey your expectations clearly to all of your supervisors so that they know what you want. Some of the items that you want to make sure the supervisors should be aware of are:

- *Attend all briefings that require their participation*

- *Be on time*

- *Be prepared to provide information on work accomplishments, remaining work, recommendations for the next operational period, estimated completion time for primary objectives, and any unusual logistical support needs*

- *Communicate performance expectations to subordinates*

- *Understand and be sensitive to political issues*

- *Make sure all operations are being conducted safely*

- *Be financially accountable for operations within their division or group; coordinate with subordinates, provide clear instructions on assignments, monitor progress, conduct follow-up upon completion of assignments*

- *Coordinate with adjacent division or group supervisors*

- *Coordinate major changes in tactics with the OSC*

- *Prepare written projection of resource needs for next operational period prior to Tactics Meeting and communicate those needs to the OSC*

- *Assess what might be demobilized without adversely impacting response operations*

☐ *Debrief at the end of each operational period. During the debriefing, verify resources and information in the IAP and update the incident map with the Situation Unit Leader*

Operations Section Chief And Deputy Operations Section Chief Duties

If you are using a Deputy OSC to help manage the Operations Section, take the time to clearly define what your duties are as the OSC and what duties you want the Deputy OSC to be responsible for. This will avoid confusion.

Below is an example to help you. In this example, the OSC has decided to work in the Incident Command Post and help the Planning Section Chief with the ICS Planning Process while the Deputy OSC is running on-scene operations.

Incident Command Post - Operations Section Chief Duties

□ Maintain constant communications with the Deputy OSC to ensure situational awareness and coordination of ICP issues

□ Ensure that Command is briefed on operational issues (common operational awareness)

□ Work with the Planning Section Chief to develop the tactical portion of the IAP

□ Working out of the ICP, coordinate with the Command and General Staff members for all planning and tactical meetings and operational briefings

□ Help to develop long-range strategic, contingency and demobilization plans

□ Help to provide operational briefings to IMT members, media and visiting dignitaries

□ Gather information from operations personnel that can be used when developing the next IAP

□ Coordinate planned activities with the Safety Officer to ensure compliance with approved safety practices

□ Coordinate with the Logistics Section on resource and logistical support issues

□ Coordinate with the Liaison Officer and Agency Representatives to assure that interagency needs are met

□ Troubleshoot operational support issues with other IMT members

□ Maintain Unit Log, ICS-214

On-Scene - Deputy Operations Section Chief Duties

- Ensure that the IAP is being effectively implemented and rapidly communicate problems back to the OSC

- Maintain effective coordination and communications with the OSC

- Oversee all activities occurring in operational area

- Be accountable for personnel and equipment assigned to the operational area

- Ensure that safe practices are being employed

- Maintain security in the operational area

- Assemble and disassemble operational elements such as task forces and strike teams as needed

- Supervise the Operations Section supervisory staff

- Reassign resources as needed

- Determine the need for additional resources

- Identify additional support facilities (e.g., Staging Areas)

- Ensure that Operations Section personnel use good safety practices

- Identify and communicate with the OSC future strategies and tactics

- Make on-scene adjustments in planned tactics

- Evaluate effectiveness of the operation

- Ensure adequate supervision is occurring

- Ensure Interagency cooperation and coordination is occurring

- Debrief off-going resources

- Keep Situation and Resources Units current on incident/resource status

- Ensure that all supervisory personnel are maintaining a Unit Log, ICS-214

Operations Section Chief Responsibilities During The Planning Meeting

The purpose of the Planning Meeting is to provide an opportunity for the OSC and the PSC to present their proposed plan of action to the IC/UC and Command and General Staff members in response to the Command's direction, objectives, and priorities that have been set for the next operational period.

□ *Review operational objectives and Command's decisions (e.g., daylight only operations) and direction*

□ *Brief on the overall strategy, tactics, and functions that will be performed to accomplish the IC/UC objectives*

□ *Review how the incident will be managed*

□ *Review work assignments and resources required*

□ *Discuss special needs (communications, facilities, security)*

□ *Discuss how Operations plans to respond to contingencies*

□ *Discuss proposed Operations Organization structure*

□ *Answer any questions and make changes to plan as needed*

Operations Section Chief Responsibilities In Reviewing The ICS-204, Assignment List

The ICS-204, Assignment List is the core of the Incident Action Plan. As the OSC, it is essential that you review each of the ICS-204s to ensure that the information on them is accurate and meets your expectations. When reviewing the ICS-204 consider the following:

- Is the information detailed enough for the field supervisors to clearly understand what work they are expected to perform?

- Are the resources listed on the ICS-204 what you had planned on the ICS-215, Operational Planning Worksheet?

- Are any special instructions that you and/or the Safety Officer wanted to note on the ICS-204 accurate and easy to understand?

- Has the Safety Officer reviewed the Assignment List?

1. BRANCH	2. ~~DIVISION~~/GROUP Search	ASSIGNMENT LIST

3. INCIDENT NAME	4. OPERATIONAL PERIOD (Date and Time)
MERIDIAN FLOOD	16 Nov 0600 to 16 Nov 1800

5. OPERATIONS PERSONNEL

OPERATIONS CHIEF __L. Hewett__   ~~DIVISION~~/GROUP SUPERVISOR __P. Robert__

BRANCH DIRECTOR _____   AIR TACTICAL GROUP SUPERVISOR _____

6. RESOURCES ASSIGNED THIS PERIOD

STRIKE TEAM/TASK FORCE RESOURCE DESIGNATOR	EMT	LEADER	NUMBER PERSONS	TRANS NEEDED	DROP OFF POINT/TIME	PICK UP POINT/TIME
MESA #3		B. Riggs	21		0530	
44120		V. Kammer	4		0530	
Ambulance #1		S. Miller	2		0530	
Helicopter 12		T. Troutman	2			

7. ASSIGNMENT

Conduct house-to-house search for injured persons. Mark each dwelling searched with a red "X" on the front door. Evacuate injured persons to triage center.

8. SPECIAL INSTRUCTIONS

Work in teams of two or more at all times. Snakes are suspected to be in the work area, wear snake gators. Personal floatation devices should be worn. Daylight operations only. Conduct regular communications checks. Send hourly updates on the group's progress to the Situation Unit.

9. DIVISION/GROUP COMMUNICATIONS SUMMARY

FUNCTION		FREQ.	SYSTEM	CHAN.	FUNCTION		FREQ.	SYSTEM	CHAN.
COMMAND	LOCAL	CDF 1	King	1	SUPPORT	LOCAL			
	REPEAT					REPEAT			
DIV./GROUP TACTICAL		157.4505	King	3	GROUND TO AIR				

PREPARED BY (RESOURCES UNIT LEADER)	APPROVED BY (PLANNING SECT. CH.)	DATE	TIME
A. Worth	J. Gafkjen	16 Nov	0400

"ICS-204 Assignment List"

OSC Readiness Checklist For the Operations Briefing

The Operations Briefing serves many purposes. Specifically it helps reduce confusion, improves communications among Operations personnel, enhances cooperation, facilitates team interaction, increases overall productivity, and ensures continuity of operations.

Remember, some people at the Operations Briefing may be new to the incident. It is absolutely critical that you present your brief such that everyone is brought up to speed. Everyone needs to be very clear on the status of the situation and what their responsibilities are for the response.

Make sure that no one is left in the dark on what has to be done and any special considerations that must be made. In preparation for the Operations Briefing ensure that you have:

- ☐ *Determined who will conduct the Operations Briefing DOSC (on-coming/off-going) or OSC (on-coming/off-going) or at least agree on who will cover what part of the material.*

- ☐ *Developed talking points to cover on-going operations (situational awareness, progress made, expectations, and any other overall issues).*

- ☐ *Identifed what will be covered in the general portion of the Operations Briefing as opposed to the DIVS specific portions.*

- ☐ *An adequate number and distribution of IAPs to the Operations attendees.*

- ☐ *Identified any last minute (pencil/ink) changes that are required of the IAP.*

- Identified a briefer that is familiar with the use/placement of visual aids.
- Evaluated the need for a public address system.
- Front row standing area during the briefing for the DIVS

Operations Briefing Checklist

The following checklist includes things that, if appropriate to the situation, should be covered in the Operations Briefing:

- Current situation
- Overall strategy and priorities
- Short and long range predictions
- Command issues
- Safety and security issues
- Medevac procedures
- Accident/injuries reporting
- Decontamination procedures
- Expected outputs and accomplishments
- Resource ordering and re-supply
- Resource status changes
- Assigned tasks and resources
- Chain of command
- Transportation issues
- Reporting time and location
- Performance expectations
- Sensitive/critical information reporting
- Updating work accomplishments
- Reporting any changes in tactics

- *Technical Specialists assigned to Operations*
- *End of shift pickup time and location*
- *Debriefing instructions*

It is easier if you break your briefing into two parts: Part One is to go over general issues that apply to everyone, and Part Two is to brief on specific issues for each individual Division, Group, or Staging Area.

Sample Operations Briefing

General Briefing Issues (part 1)

Chain of command — Make sure that everyone understands the chain of command within the Operations Section.

Resource requesting process — Tell your Branch Directors, Supervisors, and Staging Area Managers the process for how you want resources to be requested

Situation status — Report all significant changes in field conditions or occurrences through the chain of command.

Resources status — Notify your supervisor of any additional resource needs, and if the resources that are assigned to you are not appropriate for the task.

Resupply issues — Ensure that you go through your chain of command for any resupply issues.

Real time work progress reporting — When briefing your personnel, let them know who they should report work progress to and how often.

Managing critical/sensitive information — Here you want to let your field personnel know of any restrictions on how you want them to report certain information.

Accidents/injuries — Request medical assistance and then notify supervisor.

Environmental/property damage issues — Report any damage, either found or caused by incident resources to your supervisor.

End of shift debriefing process — Make sure you debrief with your relief, and after returning to the ICP, provide a full debriefing to SITL. Areas to cover in your debriefing include:

- Work accomplished — what specifically has been accomplished in your area of responsibility (e.g., number of homes searched)

- Performance issues — anything hindering performance (e.g., lack of training, personnel issues, equipment not performing as expected)

- Proper resource mix — do you need additional or different resources to complete your assignments.

- ICS-214 (Unit Log) — Fill out for each operational period.

Specific Issues (part 2)

Once you have completed your general comments, take a few minutes and make sure to go through each of the ICS-204s with the Division/Group Supervisors and Staging Area Managers. The idea here is to ensure that each supervisor or manager understands his or her assignment.

If you and Planning have done your job right, this should not take too long. The more dynamic the incident the more chance there is for confusion so make sure everyone understands their role. Consider using the incident map/chart/building plan if it helps you explain what you want done or to clarify questions. At a minimum, the briefing should cover the following on the ICS-204.

- Work assignment
- Assigned resources
- Special instructions
- Safety considerations
- Radio / telephone communications

This is the time when the supervisors and managers will ask for clarification so make sure that you respond to their questions. If you know that one of the supervisors is working in a challenging area of the response and that it will require more discussion, talk to them after the briefing so everyone else can go to work.

Daily Self-Evaluation of The Operations Section

This evaluation is internal to the Operations Section to help improve service within the Section and to the entire command team. Completion of this evaluation is the responsibility of the Operations Section Chief.

Operations Section Chief

- Are we meeting the IC/UC expectations?
- Have I provided clear direction with good follow-up?
- Is the Operations Section functioning as a team?
- Is Operations talking to the SITL with updates?
- Are we producing the highest level of quality achievable?
- Are we conducting daily Operational Briefs and Debriefs to keep things running smoothly?
- Are we conducting safe operations?
- How well does the plan reflect reality?

Operational Issues

- Do we have good familiarity of the situation on the ground; is span-of-control good?
- Are we aggressively debriefing line personnel after every operational period?
- Are we communicating with the other sections?
- Are they satisfied with our performance?
- Are tailgate safety meetings occurring?
- Are we effectively utilizing our technical specialists?
- Are we adequately staffed to support incident operations?
- Are we using General Message Forms, ICS-213?
- Do we have adequate supplies?
- Is resources status being kept up-to-date?

Personnel Issues

- Are we providing for our well-being (safety, rest, food, etc.)?
- Are ICS-214s (Unit Logs) being kept up-to-date and submitted to the DOCL?
- Are timesheets being submitted?

Demobilization Issues

- Have we thought about demobilization yet?
  - What will be the procedures?
  - What will be the priorities?
  - Have we discussed demobilization with the other Section Chiefs?

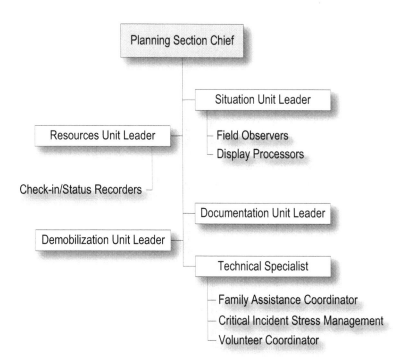

PLANNING SECTION

"Planning Section Organization"

Planning Section Chief (PSC)

The PSC, a member of the General Staff, is responsible for the collection, evaluation, dissemination, and use of incident information and maintaining status of assigned resources.

The PSC may have deputies, who may be from the same agency or from an assisting agency. The Deputy PSC must have the same qualifications as the person for whom they work, as they must be ready to take over that position at any time.

The major duties of the PSC are:

a. Review Common Responsibilities in Chapter 2

b. Collect, process, and display incident information

c. Assist OSC in the development of response strategies

d. Supervise preparation of the IAP

e. Facilitate planning meetings and briefings

f. Supervise the tracking of incident personnel and resources through the Resources Unit

g. Establish information requirements and reporting schedules for Planning Section Units (e.g., Resources, Situation)

h. Determine the need for any specialized resources in support of the incident

i. Establish special information collection activities as necessary (e.g., weather, environmental, toxics)

j. Assemble information on alternative strategies

k. Provide periodic predictions on incident potential

l. Keep IMT updated of any significant changes in incident status

m. Compile and display incident status information

n. Oversee preparation and implementation of the Incident Demobilization Plan

o. Incorporate plans (e.g., Traffic, Medical, Communications, and Site Safety) into the IAP

p. Develop incident supporting plans (e.g., security) and contingency plans (e.g., adverse weather)

q. Implement open action tracking process

r. Maintain Unit Log (ICS-214)

Situation Unit Leader (SITL)

The Situation Unit Leader is responsible for collecting, processing and organizing incident status information.

The major responsibilities of the SITL are:

a. Review Common Responsibilities in Chapter 2

b. Review Unit Leader Responsibilities in Chapter 2

c. Begin collection and analysis of incident data as soon as possible

d. Prepare, display, and disseminate incident status information

e. Prepare periodic predictions

f. Prepare the Incident Status Summary Form (ICS-209)

g. Provide maps, charts, building plans, and photographic services

h. Conduct situation briefings at meetings and briefings as required by the PSC

i. Maintain chart/map/building plans of incident in the common area of the ICP for all responders to view

j. Maintain Unit Log (ICS-214)

Field Observer (FOBS)

The FOBS is responsible for collecting situation information from personal observations at the incident and provides this information to the SITL.

The major responsibilities of the FOBS are:

a. Review Common Responsibilities in Chapter 2

b. In consultation with the SITL determine:
    - Location of assignment
    - Type of information required
    - Priorities
    - Time limits for completion
    - Method of communication
    - Method of transportation

c. Obtain necessary equipment and supplies

d. Some of the FOBS field activities include but are not limited to the following:
    - Determine the perimeter of the incident
    - Locations of trouble spots
    - Weather conditions
    - Hazards
    - Progress of operations

e. Be prepared to identify all facility locations (e.g., Helispots, Division and Branch boundaries)

f. Report information to the SITL by established procedures

g. Report immediately any condition observed that may be a safety hazard to personnel

h. Gather intelligence that will lead to accurate predictions

i. Maintain Unit Log (ICS-214)

Display Processor (DPRO)

The DPRO is responsible for the display of incident status information obtained from Field Observers (FOBS), resource status reports, aerial and other photographs, infrared data, and other sources.

The major responsibilities of the DPRO are:

a.   Review Common Responsibilities in Chapter 2

b.   In consultation with the SITL determine:
   - Location of work assignment
   - Numbers, types and locations of displays required
   - Priorities
   - Map requirements for the IAP
   - Time limits for completion

c.   Obtain necessary equipment and supplies

d.   Assist SITL in analyzing and evaluating field reports

e.   Develop required displays in accordance with time limits for completion. Examples of displays include:
   - GIS information
   - Demographic information
   - Incident projection data
   - Enlargement of ICS forms

f.   Maintain Unit Log (ICS-214)

Resources Unit Leader (RESL)

The RESL is responsible for maintaining the status of all resources on an incident. This is achieved by overseeing the check-in of all tactical resources and personnel, maintaining a status-keeping system indicating current location and status of all resources.

The major responsibilities of the RESL are:

a. Review Common Responsibilities in Chapter 2

b. Review Unit Leader Responsibilities in Chapter 2

c. Establish the check-in function at incident locations

d. Prepare Organization Assignment List (ICS-203) and Organization Chart (ICS-207)

e. Prepare appropriate parts of Assignment Lists (ICS-204)

f. Maintain and post the current status and location of all tactical resources

g. Maintain master roster of all tactical resources checked in at the incident

h. Attend meetings and briefings as required by the PSC

i. Maintain Unit Log (ICS-214)

Check-in/Status Recorder (SCKN)

SCKNs are needed at each check-in location to ensure that all resources responding to an incident are accounted for.

The major responsibilities of the SCKN are:

a. Review Common Responsibilities in Chapter 2

b. Obtain required work materials, including Check-in Lists (ICS-211), Resource Status Cards (ICS-219), or other method for tracking resources

c. Post signs so that arriving resources can easily find incident check-in location(s)

d. Record check-in information on Check-in Lists (ICS-211)

e. Transmit check-in information to the RESL

f. Forward completed (ICS-211) and Status Change Cards (ICS-210) to the RESL

g. Receive, record, and maintain resource status information on Resource Status Cards (ICS-219) for incident-assigned tactical resources, and overhead personnel

h. Maintain files of Check-in Lists (ICS-211)

i. Maintain Unit Log (ICS-214)

Documentation Unit Leader (DOCL)

The DOCL is responsible for the maintenance of accurate, up-to-date incident files. Examples of incident documentation include: Incident Action Plan(s), incident reports, communication logs, injury claims, situation status reports, etc. Thorough documentation is critical to post-incident analysis.

The DOCL shall ensure each section is maintaining and providing appropriate documents. The Documentation Unit will store incident files for legal, analytical, and historical purposes.

The major responsibilities of the DOCL are:

   a.   Review Common Responsibilities in Chapter 2

   b.   Review Unit Leader Responsibilities in Chapter 2

   c.   Set up work area; begin organization of incident documentation

   d.   Provide copying services

   e.   File all official forms and reports

   f.   Review records for accuracy and completeness; inform appropriate units of errors or omissions

   g.   Provide incident documentation as requested

   h.   Organize files for submitting final incident documentation package

   i.   Attend meetings and briefing as directed by the PSC

   j.   Maintain open action items list

   k.   Maintain Unit Log (ICS-214)

Demobilization Unit Leader (DMOB)

The DMOB is responsible for developing the Incident Demobilization Plan. On large incidents, demobilization can be quite complex, requiring a separate planning activity.

The major responsibilities of the DMOB are:

a. Review Common Responsibilities in Chapter 2

b. Review Unit Leader Responsibilities in Chapter 2

c. Review incident resource records to determine the likely size and extent of demobilization effort and develop a resource matrix

d. Coordinate demobilization with Agency Representatives

e. Monitor the on-going Operations Section resource needs

f. Identify surplus resources and probable release time

g. Establish communications with off-incident facilities, as necessary

h. Develop an incident Demobilization Plan

i. Prepare appropriate directories (e.g., maps, instructions) for inclusion in the Demobilization Plan

j. Distribute Demobilization Plan (on and off-site)

k. Ensure that all sections/units understand their specific demobilization responsibilities

l. Supervise execution of the Incident Demobilization Plan

m. Brief the PSC on demobilization progress

n. Collect lessons learned documentation for the official record

o. Maintain Unit Log (ICS-214)

Technical Specialists (THSP)

Technical Specialists provide specialized knowledge and experience that may be necessary to support incident operations. THSPs can be assigned within the Planning Section or anywhere else on the incident where their skills are needed.

The major responsibilities of the THSP are:

a. Review Common Responsibilities in Chapter 2

b. Provide technical expertise and advice to Command and General Staff

c. Develop and/or provide input into the IAP, support plan, or contingency plan

d. Attend meetings and briefings as appropriate to clarify and help to resolve technical issues within area of expertise

e. Maintain Unit Log (ICS-214)

The following are three examples of Technical Specialists that could be called on to support incident operations.

Family Assistance Coordinator

The Family Assistance Coordinator provides services to the victims' family members; coordinates activities, lodging, food, spiritual and emotional needs, and transportation to special events (e.g., press conferences, memorial services to the scene of the incident when authorized); and addresses any special needs that may assist the victims' family members.

The major responsibilities of the Family Assistance Coordinator are:

a. Review Common Responsibilities in Chapter 2

b. Coordinate with local and state authorities to include the medical examiner, local law enforcement, emergency management, hospitals, and other emergency support personnel

c. Conduct daily coordination meetings with the local and Federal government representatives to review daily activities, resolve problems, and coordinate future family support operations and activities

d. Coordinate and provide briefings to families at the incident site and those who decide not to be at the incident site

e. Ensure adequate number of Family Assistance Team members present at all times to provide the appropriate level of support to families

f. Establish and maintain working relationship with the Critical Incident Stress Management team to cross-reference needs of the survivors

g. As required, attended meetings and briefings

h. Ensure that language needs of the victims' family members are met

i. Maintain a Unit Log (ICS-214)

Critical Incident Stress Management (CISM) Specialist

The CISM Specialist is responsible for the psychological and emotional needs of all responders involved in a major incident response. The CISM Specialist is the point-of-contact for all requests from responders for CISM services and is responsible for the appropriate assignments and duties of all CISM team members.

Due to the importance of the mental well-being of all response personnel and the highly specialized nature of the CISM program, the CISM Specialist should be assigned to the command level of the ICS organization and would report directly to the Incident Commander/ Unified Command.

The major responsibilities of the CISM Specialist are:

a. Review Common Responsibilities in Chapter 2

b. Ensure there is at least one dedicated phone for CISM in the ICP

c. Determine the psychological and emotional state of the personnel involved in response and recovery operations and assess the need and level of CISM interventions

d. Ensure the Communications Unit has phone contact information for the CISM team members

e. As required, attend all staff briefings and planning meetings

f. Appropriately staff the CISM function to provide responders with timely access to CISM team members

g. Ensure that CISM team members are properly de-briefed prior to demobilizing from the incident

h. Maintain an accurate daily log of all activities including dates, times, and places where CISM activities occur

i. Maintain a Unit Log (ICS-214)

Volunteer Coordinator

The Volunteer Coordinator is responsible for managing and overseeing all aspects of volunteer participation, including recruitment, training, and deployment.

The Volunteer Coordinator is part of the Planning Section and reports to the RESL.

The major responsibilities of the Volunteer Coordinator are:

a. Review Common Responsibilities in Chapter 2

b. Coordinate with the RESL to determine the number of volunteers that are needed and any necessary skills and training needs

c. Coordinate any just-in-time training requirements and document participation

d. Maintain a list of all volunteers

e. Work with Logistics to obtain any required equipment and supplies to support the volunteer deployment.

f. Ensure that all volunteers receive a thorough briefing as to their responsibilities and the limitations and safety rules they will be working under. Document all volunteer attendance at the briefing

g. Maintain a Unit Log (ICS-214)

PLANNING SECTION CHIEF GUIDES

This Chapter is designed to help the Planning Section Chief in carrying out his or her responsibilities.

- ✓ *Planning Section Chief Briefing Checklist*
- ✓ *PSC Action and Considerations Checklist*
- ✓ *Directions to the RESL*
- ✓ *Directions to the SITL*
- ✓ *Directions to the DOCL*
- ✓ *Open Action Tracking*
- ✓ *Considerations on Demobilization*
- ✓ *Determining the Meeting Schedule*
- ✓ *Planning Section Chief role in the ICS planning process*
- ✓ *Daily Self-Evaluation of the Planning Section*

Planning Section Chief Briefing Checklist

Get a situation brief from the Incident Commander/ Unified Command (IC/UC).

This initial briefing is important and does a few things:

- You get a feel for the size and complexity of incident operations, and this helps with staffing decisions and space requirements

- You gain essential information to establish effective resources management and develop a situational status

- You assess the direction and priorities of the IC/UC

Use the following checklist to remind you of some of the more important issues and items that you should get answered during your in-brief.

At a minimum the briefing should include:

- *Incident situation: magnitude and potential of the incident*
- *Political, environmental, and economic constraints*
- *Response emphasis*
- *Facilities already established*
- *Priorities, limitations, constraints, and objectives*
- *Command structure (single or unified)*
- *Operational period and start time*
- *Hours of operation*
- *Agencies and jurisdictions involved*
- *Information on committed resources*
- *Resources ordered*
- *Media interest*
- *Incident investigation*
- *Resource requesting process*
- *Any established check-in locations*

Make sure you request a copy of the ICS-201, Incident Briefing Form, or other documents that may help you begin planning.

Planning Section Chief Action & Considerations Checklist

Once you receive your briefing it's time to establish your Planning Section. The checklist below covers some of the major actions and considerations that will get you started in the right direction. Depending on the incident, you may only use some of the items on the list.

☐ *Build your planning organization and order staff*

　☐ *Consider need for a Planning Deputy*

☐ *Establish Planning Section Incident Command Post footprint*

☐ *Brief your staff on:*

　☐ *Incident situation*

　☐ *Command objectives, priorities, limitations, and constraints*

　☐ *Work hours*

　☐ *Your expectations*

　☐ *When you need to be notified*

　☐ *What work products are expected and when you want them*

☐ *Establish check-in early at locations convenient for incoming personnel*

☐ *Start a Planning Section phone book as members of your team arrive*

☐ *Start a formal documentation process*

☐ *Determine need to assign a documentation specialist to the IC/UC to document decisions and directives*

☐ *Ensure a complete and thorough Incident Action Plan is delivered in support of the operations*

- Determine if there's a need for an ICS Technical Specialist
- Determine if there's a need to activate a volunteer coordinator position under the Resources Unit Leader
- Determine if there are any applicable contingency plans that you can use
- Determine need to develop contingency plans and functional plans
- Maintain a Unit Log, ICS-214

Directions to the Resources Unit

Time spent getting the Resources Unit established and providing critical resource information will greatly benefit the response effort. Some expectations you should set for the Resources Unit Leader.

- Ensure that check-in locations are established in the locations where the majority of resources are arriving
- Establish a Resources Status Display
- Conduct field verification of resources that arrived before check-in was set up
- Be prepared to attend the required meetings and briefings
- Ensure the resource information is as accurate as possible
- Provide maximum support to the Operations Section Chief (OSC)
- Work closely with Supply Unit Leader to ensure that the OSC resource requirements are met

Directions to the Situation Unit

A picture speaks a thousand words, and during an emergency operation the ability to rapidly communicate situational information is paramount. The priorities and objectives established by the IC/UC are grounded in their understanding of the current situation and predicted course of events.

Make sure that the Situation Unit Leader understands what you expect of them.

- Establish a master map or chart
- Establish a reporting schedule with field observers
- Ensure information is accurate and posted in a timely manner
- Displays must be neat and legible and information on the displays must be readily understood
- In addition to a master situation board, consider placing status boards at other locations such as:
  - Joint Information Center
  - Unified Command Meeting area
  - Operational Briefing area
- Deliver a situational briefing throughout the ICS Planning Process and at other times as directed
- Evaluate accuracy and verify the information you receive
- If the incident is large, consider setting up a debriefing area for overhead personnel (branch directors, supervisors, etc.) coming off the incident

Directions to the Documentation Unit

Documentation is absolutely critical. Do not let documentation of the incident be a secondary concern. Spend a few minutes with the Documentation Unit Leader and go over the following list to ensure that he or she is clear on what you expect.

- Collect pertinent documents (not an all inclusive list)
  - ICS-201, Incident Briefing Form
  - Incident Action Plans
  - Command Decisions/Directives
  - ICS-211s, Check-in Sheets
  - ICS-215s Operational Planning Worksheets
  - ICS-209s, Incident Status Summaries
  - ICS-214s, Unit Logs
- Ensure that any documentation that is submitted to the Documentation Unit is accurate and complete. If not, work with the submitting party to correct errors or omissions
- Obtain PSC approval prior to the release of any incident-related documentation or reports
- Establish incident files; ensure that the PSC and the DOCL agree on a particular filing system to use for the incident to ensure continuity and to avoid confusion later on. Filing system options include:
  - File by operational period
  - File by calendar date
  - File by form number
- Attend meetings
  - Unified Command Objectives Meeting
  - Command and General Staff Meeting
  - Planning Meeting
- Maintain open action tracking

Open Action Tracking

As the Planning Section Chief, make sure that you have established an open action tracking system to record any tasking the IC/UC may assign to the Incident Management Team. Someone should be assigned to complete each item on the list. Review the open action tracking list at subsequent meetings to ensure that the tasks are completed.

Below are a few examples of open actions:

- Establish a Joint Information Center by 9:00 am (PIO)
- Bring in a Critical Incident Stress Management Team (PSC)
- Develop a Site Safety Plan (SOF)

Considerations on Demobilization

Efficient demobilization can only occur with some forethought and good planning. Here are a few thoughts on demobilization.

- Start planning early
- Recognize the indicators to begin demobilization
  - No new resources ordered
  - End of incident is in sight
  - There are unassigned resources
- Ensure that the Demobilization Unit Leader (DMOB) is getting the support he or she needs from the entire command team

Determining the Meeting Schedule

Once the time for the next operational period is set, the Planning Section Chief will determine the times that certain steps in the ICS Planning Process should occur. This is necessary to ensure that all steps are accomplished and that an IAP is ready for the IC/UC approval in time to begin the operational period.

If the start of the operational period is 1800 (6:00 pm), the Planning Section Chief works backward from 1800 to determine when each step in the planning process needs to start.

Below is an example that you can use to help determine when the various meetings and briefings should take place.

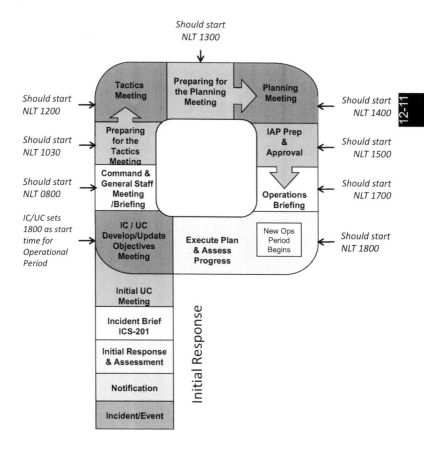

"Determining the meeting schedule"

Planning Section Chief Role in the ICS Planning Process

ICS-201, Incident Briefing

The ICS-201, Incident Briefing, is an important but informal briefing with no established agenda with the exception of following the format of the ICS-201 form. However, the intent of the ICS-201 briefing is to ensure an orderly transfer of command when a more qualified person arrives on-scene to assume command of the incident. The main player at this briefing is the initial response Incident Commander who will conduct the briefing to the incoming IC or Unified Command. Some of your specific responsibilities as the PSC are to:

- *Facilitate the ICS-201 brief*
- *If possible, provide a copy of the ICS-201 to attendees*
- *Document discussion points, concerns, and open action items*
- *Distribute a copy of the ICS-201 to RESL and SITL*

Initial Unified Command Meeting (held only once)

The Initial Unified Command Meeting agenda will cover a wide range of issues that the UC will need to come to agreement on, such as which agency will provide the Operations Section Chief, the length of the operational period, and many other issues. At a minimum, what you need to come away with from the meeting are:

- *A good set of objectives and priorities*
- *Operational period duration (e.g., 12 hours, 24 hours) and start time (e.g., 6:00 AM, 12:00 PM)*
- *Unified Command's expectations of the Incident Management Team*
- *Documentation of the UC decisions, including limitations and constraints*

Unified Command Develop/Update Objectives Meeting

As the PSC, you should personally attend this meeting and take notes on the Unified Commanders' decisions and tasking and provide an update on any open action items. Following this meeting you should:

- *Brief the Planning Section staff on objectives and decisions*
- *Provide documentation to the Documentation Unit Leader (DOCL)*
- *Have the Situation Unit Leader post objectives and decisions*
- *Prepare for the Command and General Staff Meeting*

Command and General Staff Meeting

When facilitating this meeting, you need to be flexible with the agenda as it might change from meeting to meeting based on the desires of the IC/UC. It's important to capture decisions and directives and display them in the ICP. Some example decisions might be:

- The UC will review and approve all media information dissemination
- 24-hour operational period will be used running from 0600 to 0600
- The OSC will be the local fire department chief

As the PSC, it is your responsibility to:

☐ *Facilitate the meeting*

☐ *Document any work tasks and note who is responsible for completing them*

☐ *Resolve conflicts and clarify roles and responsibilities before meeting is adjourned*

☐ *Brief the Planning Section staff*

☐ *Provide documentation to the DOCL*

Preparing for the Tactics Meeting

During the time between the Command and General Staff Meeting and the Tactics Meeting, the Operations Section Chief (OSC) should be thinking about, and developing, a rough draft of his/her tactical plan in support of the objectives for the next operational period.

You want to help the OSC put together the plan of action that he/she will present at the Tactics Meeting.

You'll want to ensure that the Safety Officer also provides input on the chosen tactics. To do that:

□ *Meet with the OSC to discuss his or her strategies (how he's going to accomplish an objective) and the tactical plan (the equipment and personnel he requires to actually implement the strategy)*

□ *Help the Operations Section Chief fill in the Operational Planning Worksheet, ICS-215*

□ *Ensure that the Safety Officer reviews the proposed tactics*

Tactics Meeting

Although the Tactics Meeting is driven by an agenda and kept on track by the PSC, it's an informal meeting between the participants to help the OSC develop or refine a workable tactical plan that meets the IC/UC objectives.

As the PSC, it's your job to ensure that this meeting occurs on time and that the following items are completed before the meeting adjourns:

- *Completed draft of the Operational Planning Worksheet, ICS- 215*

- *Operations Organization is identified and drawn out*

- *Any logistical requirements are identified*

- *The Safety Officer has worked with the OSC to identify and mitigate any safety concerns*

- *The OSC's tactical plan has been "scrubbed" against the IC/UC objectives and priorities to ensure no objective was overlooked*

Preparing for the Planning Meeting

Consult the list below to ensure that the Planning Section is prepared to support the Planning Meeting.

☐ *The meeting time and location have been communicated to participants*

☐ *Is the meeting room ready (seating, signs, displays, audio-visuals, other support materials, etc...)?*

☐ *Do meeting attendees understand their roles and responsibilities during the meeting?*

☐ *Has the meeting time and location been posted/ advertised?*

☐ *Have the necessary handouts and other meeting support materials been reproduced and distributed?*

☐ *Is the Situation Unit Leader prepared and ready to conduct the situation briefing along with projections and/or forecasts? Has the SITL coordinated with others that will be briefing (e.g., Technical Specialist)?*

☐ *Are the wall displays needed by the OSC ready and in the proper order?*

☐ *Have you, the PSC, met with the Command to discuss meeting protocols (e.g., facilitation,) and to determine any requirements that the Command may have (e.g., talking points)?*

☐ *Is the Documentation Unit Leader/Recorder briefed and ready to document the meeting, including any open action items?*

Planning Meeting

If you've prepared right, there should never be any surprises during this meeting. You want the IC/UC to see a united team that can support the Operations Section Chief's tactical plan for the next operational period. It's at this meeting that:

- Final touches are put on the ICS-215
- The IC/UC gives provisional approval of the plan
- You obtain concurrence from the Command and General Staff that they can support the plan
- You confirm the availability of resources
- You document decisions and any tasking by the IC/UC

Incident Action Plan Preparation

As the PSC, you're responsible for supervising the preparation of the IAP, and ensuring that all components of the IAP are completed. This requires working with the:

- Safety Officer
- Communications Unit Leader
- Medical Unit Leader
- Situation Unit Leader
- Resources Unit Leader
- Documentation Unit Leader
- Operations Section Chief

After the IAP is complete:

- *Review the completed IAP for correctness*

- *Provide the IAP to IC/UC for review and approval*

- *Once approved, have copies of the signed IAP made in preparation for the Operations Briefing*

- *Provide the DOCL with the original signed IAP for inclusion into the permanent incident record*

Is the Planning Section ready for the Operations Briefing

To ensure that the Operations Briefing runs smoothly use the checklist below to determine if the Planning Section is ready to facilitate a professional briefing.

- *The meeting time and location have been communicated to participants*

- *All materials are prepared and available to support the briefing*

- *Briefing area is properly prepared to conduct the briefing*

- *All Command and General Staff members have been reminded to have their talking points ready*

- *All displays are in place and legible (e.g., large wall displays)*

- *Any last minute changes to the IAP have been identified and are ready to be briefed*

- *The Situation Unit Leader's briefing is focused toward the field personnel (e.g., supervisors, leaders, staging area managers)*

- *If appropriate, is security prepared to control access to the briefing area*

Operations Briefing

The quality of this briefing is primarily dependent on the OSC, but you as the PSC will help to ensure that the briefing goes smoothly:

❑ *Distribute a copy of the IAP to each branch director, division/group supervisor, staging area manager, and others with field supervisory assignment responsibilities*

❑ *Document any changes to the IAP made at the briefing*

Execute Plan and Assess Progress

Once the operational period starts, the plan outlined in the IAP must be constantly assessed to ensure that it still meets the actual situation on the ground. Should the OSC adjust the plan, ensure that any critical changes are communicated to those who need to track them. For example:

▪ The IC/UC for changes in the tactical plan that will delay completing objectives

▪ The Resources Unit for any changes in a resource's location or status

▪ The Situation Unit for any observed changes in the situation that were not anticipated

Daily Self-evaluation of the Planning Section

This evaluation is internal to the Planning Section and serves to help improve service within the Section and to the entire command team. Completion of this evaluation is the responsibility of the Planning Section Chief.

Planning Section Chief

- Is the Planning Section being the leader on this incident in ICS management?

- Have I (PSC) provided clear direction with good follow-up?

- Is the Planning Section functioning as a team?

- Is the Planning space neat and orderly?

- Are we producing the highest level of quality achievable?

- Are we conducting daily Planning Section meetings to discuss internal issues?

Planning Issues

- Do we have good familiarity with the situation on the ground?

- Are reporting deadlines established and being met?

- Are we aggressively debriefing off-going branch directors and division/group supervisors (DIVS) after every operational period?

- Are we communicating with the other Sections?

- Are they satisfied with our performance?

- Has a meeting schedule been developed?

- Are we effectively utilizing our technical specialists?

- Are we adequately staffed to support incident operations?

- Is there a documentation filing system set up?
- Do we have adequate supplies?
- Is resources status being kept up-to-date?
- Is the Documentation Unit being fully supported by the entire command team?
- Are the situational displays up-to-date?
- Are we delivering a quality IAP?

Personnel Issues

- Are we providing for our well-being (safety, rest, food, etc.)?
- Are ICS-214s (Unit Logs) being kept up-to-date?
- Are timesheets being submitted?

Demobilization Issues

Have we thought about demobilization yet?

- What will be the procedures?
- What will be the priorities?
- Have we discussed demobilization with the other Section Chiefs?

SITUATION UNIT LEADER GUIDES

This Chapter assists the Situation Unit Leader in carrying out his or her responsibilities. The following guides are included:

✓ *Situation Unit Leader In-brief Checklist*

✓ *Situation Unit Staffing Guidelines*

✓ *Sample Instructions to the Field Observer (FOBS)*

✓ *Map / Chart symbology*

✓ *Wildland Fire Symbology*

✓ *Oil Spill Symbology*

✓ *Miscellaneous Symbols*

✓ *Establishing Situation Display*

✓ *Map Display*

✓ *Sample Traffic Plan*

✓ *Information Dissemination*

✓ *Best Briefing Practices*

Situation Unit Leader In-Brief Checklist

After arriving at the incident and checking in, you need to find the Planning Section Chief or the Incident Commander, if the PSC has not arrived on-scene, and get a briefing.

This briefing is critical. Without it you'll be wasting precious time in establishing your unit. The bottom line is to get enough detail so that you can develop an accurate picture of the current situation.

Some of the information you'll need to get from your briefing is provided in the checklist below.

- ☐ *Current situation*
- ☐ *Incident potential*
- ☐ *Location of any incident facilities (e.g., Helispots)*
- ☐ *Incident objectives*
- ☐ *Establishment of any Divisions, Groups, Branches*
- ☐ *Weather information*
- ☐ *Meeting schedule*

Make sure you request a copy of the ICS-201, Incident Briefing Form (pages 1 and 2) or other documents that may help you begin to develop an accurate situational picture.

Situation Unit Staffing Guidelines

There are no "hard-and-fast" rules on staffing the Situation Unit. When you try to determine the number of Field Observers you need to take into account the number of Divisions/Groups where the situation is dynamic and where there is a lack of situational information.

If the situation is stable, one Field Observer may be able to cover several Divisions/Groups. As for the number of Display Processors, you need enough of them to keep up with the incoming information. Technical Specialists can range from none to numerous, based on the type of incident and its complexity.

Take into account the following variables as you make your best determination of what personnel you'll need to have an effective unit. These variables include:

- Intensity of the operations being conducted
- Size of the incident (is there a large command team in place)
- Complexity of the incident (may require many technical specialists)
- Duration of the incident (need to factor into your staffing needs the ability to manage the Situation Unit 24 hours-a-day, 7 days-a-week)
- Number of locations where situation displays are maintained
- Information demand

Sample Instructions to the Field Observer (FOBS)

We recommend that you create written instructions for the FOBS to help guide their actions and to ensure that the FOBS understand what you expect of them. Below is a sample of written instructions to the FOBS. Much of the information that is in the sample instruction applies to any type of incident.

General Information

- Establish contact with the field supervisor(s) whose area(s) you are working in

- Discuss with the field supervisor your information reporting requirements

- Do not go into any areas where there is not adequate communications (you must be able to have communications with someone on the incident)

- Ensure that have you have read and initialed the Site Safety Plan and adhere to the Plan's requirements

- Ensure that you have the contact information for the field supervisors whose area you will be operating in

- Ensure that all equipment is in working order before going into the field (e.g., communications equipment, safety equipment, GPS, cameras, binoculars)

- Ensure that you have a copy of the incident map/charts to use as common references when reporting information back to the Situation Unit

- Return all non-expendable equipment

- Ensure that you have the right clothing for predicted weather conditions

- Have on hand adequate water and food for the estimated time you will be in the field

- Make sure that you have coordinated your transportation requirements with Logistics

- Use common map references (latitude and longitude) when communicating back to the Situation Unit

Information to Collect

- Safety hazards (Safety Officer)
  - Power lines (lying across access roads)
  - Hazardous materials
  - Unique weather conditions (ice, fog)
  - Topography (steep slope, narrow canyons)
  - Water conditions (swift current, extreme tides)
- Discrepancies in resource deployment based on the IAP (RESL)
- Transportation (GSUL)
  - Condition of roads within the incident area (e.g., bridge limited to 5,000 lbs, traffic choke points)
- Work Accomplished
  - Measurement of fire line production
  - Amount of boom deployed and location
  - Status of mitigation activities (e.g., chlorine release secured, hole in levee wall 50% filled)
- Impacts of the incident on:
  - Transportation infrastructure
  - Wildlife
  - Commercial and private property
  - Historic properties
  - Cultural sites
  - Hindrances (e.g., private property)
- Amount and location of shoreline contaminated
- Impact of the response efforts on the environment (e.g., improper disposal of contaminated debris)
- Any suspicious activities
- Any spontaneous special interest group activities (e.g., they may be in harms way)
- Validate prediction modeling
- Conduct weather observations (requires weather kit)
- Any established or potential sites for support facilities (e.g., helispots)

Report-in times

- You are to regularly report in to the Situation Unit and provide updates (e.g., every hour)

Map/Chart Symbology

One method of communicating incident information is through the symbols used on maps or charts. Below are the most common symbols used.

RED

⊗ **31 Dec 1530**
Hazard Origin (Include date and time)

Four Corners ◢
Incident Command Post (Designated by name of the incident)

H-4 ⬤
Helispots (Designated by number)

BLUE

4th Street Staging Ⓢ
Staging Areas (Designated by their general location)

Four Corners Helibase Ⓗ
Helibase (Designated by name of the incident)

Four Corners Base Ⓑ
Incident Base (Designated by incident name)

Mills Camp Ⓒ
Camp (Designated by geographic name or number)

BLACK

Division Boundary Y̲

(A) (B)
Divisions (initially lettered clockwise from incident origin)
Divisions are designated by letters of the alphabet: A, B, C, etc.

Branch Boundary)(

[I] [II]
Branches (initially numbered clockwise from incident origin)
Branches are designated by Roman Numerals: I, II, III, etc.

East 7kts
➡
1600 12/31
Wind Direction and Speed (note time and date, e.g., 1600 12/31)

"Common ICS Symbols"

Wildland Fire Symbology

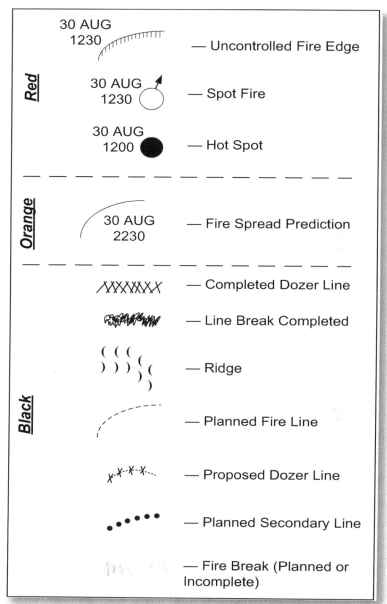

Red

30 AUG 1230 — Uncontrolled Fire Edge

30 AUG 1230 — Spot Fire

30 AUG 1200 — Hot Spot

Orange

30 AUG 2230 — Fire Spread Prediction

Black

XXXXXXXX — Completed Dozer Line

— Line Break Completed

(((( ))) ( ) — Ridge

— Planned Fire Line

x-x-x-x... — Proposed Dozer Line

•••••• — Planned Secondary Line

— Fire Break (Planned or Incomplete)

"Common wildland firefighting symbols"

Oil Spill Symbology

These symbols are recommended for placement on the overlays used over the base chart(s). These symbols should be placed on the overlays using the color black.

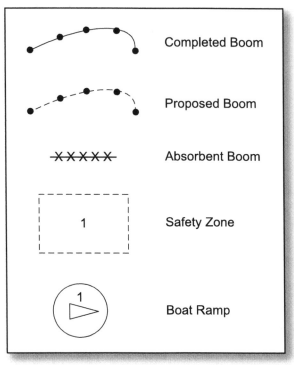

"Symbols that can be used during an oil spill response"

Miscellaneous Symbols

These symbols are recommended for placement on the base map, chart, or building plans. These symbols should be placed using the color black.

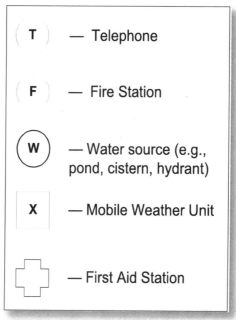

"Additional symbols that can be used to communicate information to responders'

Establishing Situation Display

Below is an example of how you might consider setting up your displays. The displays should be established in a manner that lets anyone examining them to quickly capture the information. That said, access to update the displays should be limited to Situation Unit personnel. These displays serve the responders and are a part of the historical record of what transpired on the incident.

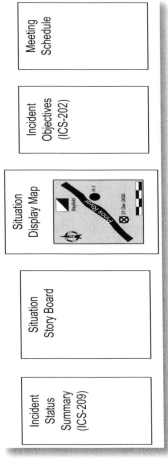

"Example situation display layout"

Map Display

The maps/charts the Situation Unit produces must help responders to do their job and the more detailed your displays are for their area of operations, the better. When establishing and maintaining your maps, charts, building plans, etc. consider the following:

- Strive for a high-quality presentation
- Ensure accuracy of situational information
- Maintain current information
- Establish a method to capture map/chart information for historical purposes

Use the memory-jogger "STAND" to help ensure the maps and charts have the required information.

S — Show the scale. Hand-drawn maps not to scale should be annotated with the words "Not to Scale."

T — Place a title on the map. The map should be titled with its use (e.g., Incident Map)

A —The author's name should appear on the map

N — The map should show a north arrow

D — The map should show the date and time when the information was gathered (e.g., the chart was last updated on 2 August 0800)

Opposite is an example of an incident map using the STAND criteria.

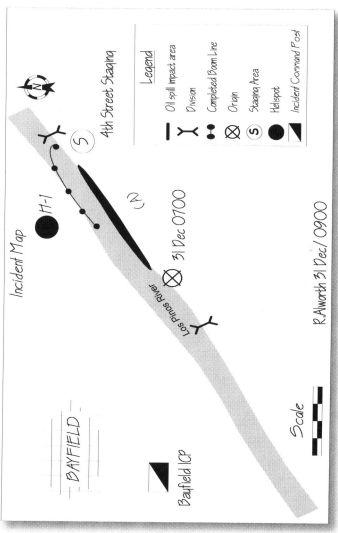

Incident Map

Legend

Oil spill impact area	|
Division	⅄
Completed Boom Line	•••
Origin	⊗
Staging Area	(S)
Helspot	●
Incident Command Post	◤

4th Street Staging

H-1

31 Dec 0700

Los Pinos River

R.Aworth 31 Dec / 0900

Scale

BAYFIELD

Bayfield ICP

"The use of common ICS terminology extends to the symbols used on maps and charts"

13-15

Sample Traffic Plan

The Traffic Plan is prepared to assist resources in getting to their assignments. This is usually a hand drawn map, but may be a copy of a local road map. Specifics to the Traffic Map include:

- Keep to one page if possible
- May add narrative directions to complement the map
- Map should include access to and from incident facilities
- One-way roads should be indicated
- Routes requiring 4-wheel drive should be noted

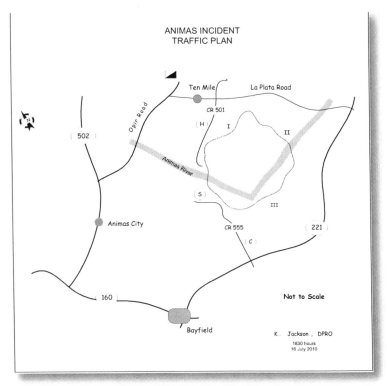

"Example of a Traffic Plan"

Information Dissemination

You should use all avenues at your disposal to push information out to the Incident Management Team. In addition to the large wall displays, you should use inboxes/outboxes (like those used on a person's work desk) for getting information out to the team, collecting information, and for placing historical records that the Documentation Unit will require.

Boxes identified for distributing information might contain:

- 8.5 x 11-inch copies of the most recent incident map
- Future weather, tides, and sunrise/sunset
- Extra Incident Action Plans
- Meeting schedule

Boxes identified for collecting information might contain:

- Field Observer reports

Boxes identified for historical records might contain:

- Completed ICS-214, Unit Logs
- Annotated maps/charts
- ICS-209, Incident Status Summary
- Photographs

Best Briefing Practices

Consider the following practices if you're preparing and/or presenting a briefing.

As the Briefer:

- *Plan ahead by arranging your source and display material in a logical sequence or use provided format that is expected and is easily understood*

- *At the start of your briefing ensure that you professionally introduce yourself. Your briefing should include:*
  - *The time and date the briefing material covers*
  - *Title of the briefing (e.g., Planning Meeting)*
  - *Incident situation, area impacted, any new support facilities established*
  - *Impact to infrastructure, modes of transportation (e.g., road closures)*
  - *Number of injured and fatalities*
  - *Success of mitigation efforts (e.g., 50% of buildings searched, 8 miles of shoreline boomed)*
  - *Major considerations (e.g., weather, tides and currents, high priority activities, political sensitivities)*
  - *Forecast, predictions, trajectories*

- *Understand the target audience for the briefing and tailor the briefing to meet the information requirement*
  - *If audience is mixed agency/organizations, avoid acronyms*

- *Anticipate potential questions in advance and have the answers ready. If you don't know the answer to a question, say you don't know and make note of the question for prompt follow-up. DOCL should be capturing open issues.*

□ Check the presentation area for lighting, display area, seating, and size for the anticipated audience

□ Review preparations with the Planning Section Chief for advice and guidance

□ Contact the key presenter (e.g., OSC) informally prior to getting together to make sure that there is a clear understanding of who will be briefing what material so that the briefing is coordinated

□ Determine in-advance if material to be discussed is of a sensitive nature and if so, limit attendance according to presenter's direction

□ Speak in a strong, well-modulated voice and avoid distracting mannerisms

□ Ensure you know how the Planning Section Chief wants to work questions and answers (Q & A). Will Q & A be allowed during the briefing or following

□ Use presentation technology (e.g., PowerPoint) as appropriate and only if you have mastered it. You do not want the briefer or the technology to distract from the presentation

□ At the end, summarize key points as necessary

Supporting Material:

- All display and handout material must have a date and time shown along with the person's name that prepared and/or approved the material

- If you're using audio/visual material have spare bulbs, cords, handouts and other material that might fail or not be sufficient for extra attendees

- If you're using wall displays that might be hard to read, then provide duplicates in smaller sizes for key attendees

DOCUMENTATION UNIT LEADER GUIDES

This Chapter is designed to help the Documentation Unit Leader in carrying out his or her responsibilities. The following guides are included:

✓ *Arriving On-scene as the Documentation Unit Leader*

✓ *Documentation Unit Staffing Chart*

✓ *Assessing the Status of Incident Documentation*

✓ *Some Best Practices*

Arriving On-scene as the Documentation Unit Leader

One of the first responsibilities you have after checking-in to the incident is to receive an in-briefing from the PSC. This briefing will give you a sense for how complex the documentation effort is going to be. It's during this briefing that you should:

- Discuss with the PSC his/her expectations for incident documentation
  - Confirm what meetings and briefings the PSC would like you to attend. These meetings include:
    - Unified Command Develop / Update Objectives Meeting
    - Command and General Staff Meeting
    - Planning Meeting
  - Clarify the DOCL authority to release any incident-related documentation or reports to anyone outside of the Command and General Staff
  - Determine how the PSC would like the filing system for the incident to be established
    - File by operational period
    - File by calendar date
    - File by form number
- Determine where the Documentation Unit is to be located
- Find out from the PSC what documentation efforts have been undertaken and where collected documents are located (retrieve those documents as soon as you can since they will be your starting place)

❑ Ask the PSC if there are any additional requirements that the Documentation Unit is expected to perform Examples of additional duties may include:

> ❑ Photo documentation of the incident

> ❑ Providing copies of archived documents to outside requesters, responding to Freedom of Information Act (FOIA)

Documentation Unit Staffing Chart

Although there are no established guidelines for staffing the Documentation Unit, you can use a table like the example below to help you determine the level of support that you'll require to accomplish your responsibilities.

List the various tasks that your unit has to perform and the different skills that you'll need to accomplish those tasks. One thing to keep in mind as you're developing your staffing is that you may have to staff the Documentation Unit 24-hours a day during the height of the response. So remember to factor that into your staffing determinations.

Tasking	Administration Assistant	Photo Documentation	Note Taker
Filing	2		
Copy/Fax	1		
Meeting Documentation			1
Photo Management		1	

"Documentation Unit staffing table"

Assessing the Status of Incident Documentation

If you're the first Documentation Unit Leader at the incident, you're going to have a big job ahead of you. While you are waiting for the staff that you ordered to arrive, conduct an assessment on the status of the incident documentation efforts that are currently underway. Your assessment should at least focus on the following:

- ❑ Determine how incident documentation is currently being collected and identify gaps in the collection process

    - ❑ A good example of a time-critical documentation gap is information that is leaving the Incident Command Post (ICP) via e-mail or facsimile

- ❑ Determine what can be done to close any identified gaps immediately and take those steps, even if the solution is only a short-term measure

- ❑ At an absolute minimum, determine if the following documents are being collected, and, if not, start collecting them. Always try to get the originals for the incident files.

    - ❑ ICS-201, Incident Briefing Form

    - ❑ IAPs with original signatures (number pages of the IAP: e.g., 1 of 22; 2 of 22; 3 of 22 for continuity)

    - ❑ Command decisions/directives

    - ❑ Site Safety Plan (SSP) with original signature (number pages of the SSP: e.g., 1 of 22; 2 of 22; 3 of 22 for continuity)

    - ❑ Signature sheets of those who reviewed the Site Safety Plan

    - ❑ Contingency and other non-IAP plans with original signatures

    - ❑ Press releases

- ICS-211, Check-in sheets
- ICS-215, Operational Planning Worksheets
- ICS-209, Incident Status Summaries
- ICS-214, Unit Logs (everyone's)

☐ Determine if there are important meetings taking place that are outside the normal planning process and assess if someone from Documentation Unit should attend and record important decisions or discussions

☐ If there is a Legal Officer attached to the command team, discuss with the officer any documentation requirements that he or she may have

Some Best Practices

☐ Introduce yourself to the Command and General Staff and let each of them know what your incident-documentation needs are and ask for their support. Encourage them to emphasize to the members on their individual staffs the importance of thorough documentation

☐ Encourage everyone on the Command and General Staff to keep records in writing of their critical decisions and issues. The ICS-214 was developed to capture this information, but any pad of paper will do the trick. The bottom line is that the key players on the incident command team need to keep a running log of their activities

☐ Talk to the PSC about having the IC/UC make incident documentation a discussion issue during the next Command and General Staff Meeting

☐ Consider having a member of your Documentation Unit staff assigned to the Unified Command to ensure that formal documentation of decisions are captured and recorded

DEMOBILIZATION UNIT LEADER GUIDES

If you're called to an incident to assume the responsibilities of Demobilization Unit Leader, you will be stepping into a very dynamic environment and you must move rapidly once you have checked into the incident to get up-to-speed and develop an effective demobilization plan. The guides below will help you get started in the right direction.

✓ *Arriving On-scene as the Demobilization Unit Leader*

✓ *Building a Demobilization Plan*

✓ *Steps in the Demobilization Process*

✓ *Demobilization Resource Tracking System*

Arriving On-scene as the Demobilization Unit Leader

Your challenge once you have checked into the incident is to get a feel for the size and complexity of the demobilization effort. To help accomplish this:

- *Obtain a briefing from the Planning Section Chief to get an idea on the scope of the demobilization and to determine how much time you have to establish the Demobilization Unit before resources start demobilizing*

- *Review incident documents/databases*
    - *ICS-201, Incident Briefing Form, (initial response resources may have not been captured during check-in)*
    - *ICS-211, Check-in Form(s)*
    - *Incident Action Plans*
    - *T-cards (what resources are currently assigned and where they are)*
    - *Computer databases used to track resources*

- *Meet with the Resources Unit Leader to get his/her thoughts on demobilization*

In addition to the RESL, the entire Command and General Staff and others (e.g., Time Unit) are there to support your efforts.

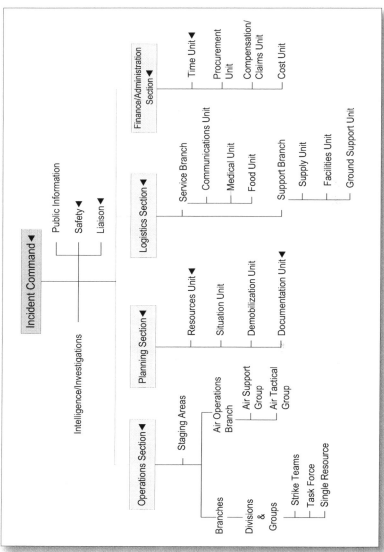

◀ICS positions the DMOB will interact with during an incident

Building a Demobilization Plan

Demobilization Plans generally follow the same format, but you'll see variances based on who is generating the plan, the type of incident the plan is supporting, and other nuances unique to the particular agencies involved. Regardless, all Demobilization Plans should contain the following to be effective:

General Information Section — (this section should be short but informative) and include:

- Incident Commander/Unified Command expectations
- Safety considerations
- Directions to the Section Chiefs
- Description of the demobilization procedures

Responsibilities Section — (this section establishes position specific demobilization responsibilities) for example:

- Planning Section Chief
  - Ensures demobilization information is provided to the response organization in sufficient time to conduct an orderly downsizing of incident resources
  - Submits proposed release of resources to the Incident Commander (IC)/Unified Command (UC) for approval
  - Ensures released resources follow established demobilization procedures
- Operations Section Chief
  - Identifies and communicates excess personnel and equipment available for demobilization to the Planning Section Chief (Operations Section is the biggest customer of demobilization since they have the bulk of the resources)

- Logistics Section Chief
  - Coordinates all personnel and equipment transportation needs to their final destination
  - Ensures property accountability for all nonconsumable items (e.g., fire hose, radios)
- Finance/Administration Section Chief ensures completion of:
  - Time records (personnel and equipment)
  - Injury reports
  - Claim reports
- Safety Officer reviews plan for health and safety issues
  - Ensures drivers have adequate sleep before driving to their final destination
  - Verifies personnel tracking system is in place and being used to ensure responders have arrived at their destination safely
- Liaison Officer
  - Coordinates with assisting organizations demobilization information of their resources

Release Priorities

- The Incident Commander/Unified Command will determine the release priorities taking into consideration
  - Ongoing incident resource requirements
  - Personnel welfare (safety and rest)
  - Needs of the responding agencies
  - Home unit of the resource (out-of-area or local)
  - Resource cost

Release Procedures

- Procedures to be followed for obtaining release

Phone Directory

- Include important contact numbers for the DMOB process (e.g., DMOB, EOC)

Steps in the Demobilization Process

Once the Demobilization Plan has been approved by the IC/UC, the demobilization process begins. Below are the steps that should be followed in order to ensure the orderly release of resources.

Step 1 — All unit leaders in Planning, Logistics, and Finance/Administration identify any surplus resources at least 24 hours in advance of their anticipated demobilization time. The Resources Unit Leader will work with the Operations Section Chief to identify Operation's surplus resources

Step 2 — Lists of identified surplus resources for each Section are given to the Section Chief who will forward the tentative list of surplus resources to the Planning Section Demobilization Unit

Step 3 — The Demobilization Unit will compile a tentative list of surplus resources from all Sections and send them to the Incident Commander/Unified Command via the Planning Section Chief

Step 4 — Incident Commander/Unified Command approves the list of resources to be demobilized

Step 5 — Approved demobilization list is sent to the Resources Unit and to the LSC and any other appropriate Section Chiefs

The following is an example of a Tentative Release List Form.

TENTATIVE RELEASE LIST

From: _____ (Section Chief or Command Staff Officer)

The following resources are surplus as of _____ (hours) on _____ (date). At that time, these resources are available for release processing.

	Name of Individual, Crew, or Equipment in excess	Position on the Incident
1	Patrick Robert	Supervisor
2		
3		
4		
5		
6		
7		
8		
9		
10		
11		
12		
13		
14		
15		
16		
17		
18		
19		
20		

_____
Signature of Section Chief or Command Staff Officer
Date: _____ Time: _____

"Tentative Release List used by the Command and General Staff to identify recommended resources for demobilization"

Step 6 — Section Chiefs notify the resources under their control that they have been approved for demobilization and what procedures they should follow

Step 7— Demobilization Unit ensures that the checkout process is followed

Step 8 — Demobilization Unit sends completed Demobilization Checkout forms, ICS-221, to the Documentation Unit for the historical record. Each resource that demobilizes from the incident will complete the ICS-221

The following is an example of a Demobilization Checkout Form.

DEMOBILIZATION CHECKOUT		ICS-221
1. INCIDENT NAME/NUMBER Meridian Flood	2. DATE/TIME 27 Nov 1800	3. DEMOB NUMBER
4. UNIT/PERSONNEL RELEASED Patrick Robert		
5. TRANSPORTATION TYPE/NUMBER Commercial Air (see block 12 for additional information)		
6. ACTUAL RELEASE DATE/TIME 28 Nov 0900	7. Manifest YES NO NO	
8. DESTINATION Arcata, California	9. AREA/AGENCY/REGION NOTIFIED Region IX notified on 27 Nov 2000	
10. UNIT LEADER RESPONSIBLE FOR COLLECTING PERFORMANCE RATING Not required by Agency		

11. UNIT/PERSONNEL YOU AND YOUR RESOURCES HAVE BEEN RELEASED SUBJECT TO SIGNOFF FROM THE FOLLOWING:
(DMOB UNIT LEADER CHECK BOXES THAT APPLY)

LOGISTICS SECTION

- [X] SUPPLY UNIT
- [X] COMMUNICATIONS UNIT
- [ ] FACILITIES UNIT
- [ ] GROUND SUPPORT UNIT

PLANNING SECTION

- [ ] DOCUMENTATION UNIT

FINANCE/ADMINISTRATION SECTION

- [X] TIME UNIT

OTHER

- [X] SAFETY OFFICER

12. Remarks
   Frontier Airlines flight 271

"The Demobilization Checkout Form, ICS-221, is used to ensure the orderly release of resources."

Demobilization Resource Tracking System

To help you keep track of the status of demobilizing resources, consider developing a demobilization tracking table (opposite page).

Your goal is to be able to accurately track the movement of resources as they leave the incident. The table you create will be a big help to the Safety Officer because he/she can use it to ensure that drivers are not leaving the incident before they get adequate rest.

Demobilization Resource Tracking Table

Agency	Name	Order #	Check-In	Last Shift	Sent Home	Home Base	Assignment	Travel
BFD	Patrick Robert	0-020	15-Nov	27-Nov	28-Nov	Arcata, CA	DIVS	Air
BFD	Scott Kelly	0-004	15-Nov	27-Nov	28-Nov	Bayfield, CO	STAM	POV
ANF	Jack Voelker	0-008	15-Nov	27-Nov	28-Nov	Bayfield, CO	THSP	POV
USCG	Mary Yale	0-012	15-Nov	27-Nov	27-Nov	Durango, CO	IC	GOV
FBI	John Murry	0-022	16-Nov	28-Nov	29-Nov	Cortez, CO	PSC	GOV

"Using a demobilization resource tracking table can greatly facilitate maintaining an accurate and efficient demobilization process"

RESOURCES UNIT LEADER GUIDES

This Chapter is designed to help the Resources Unit Leader in carrying out his or her responsibilities.

- ✓ *Resources Unit Leader In-brief Checklist*
- ✓ *Determine the Resources Unit Staffing Needs*
- ✓ *Check-in form (ICS-211)*
- ✓ *Determine Resources Already in the Field (field verification)*
- ✓ *T-Card System (tracking incident resources)*
- ✓ *Establishing a Resources Status Display Using T-Cards*
- ✓ *Resource Assignment Flowchart During an Operational Period*
- ✓ *RESL Support to the Tactics Meeting*
- ✓ *The ICS-204 Assignment List*
- ✓ *The ICS-203 Organization Assignment List*
- ✓ *Resources Unit Leader Involvement in Demobilization*

Resources Unit Leader In-brief Checklist

One of the most important things that the RESL can do to get a good start on establishing an effective Resources Unit is to get as detailed a briefing as possible when you report to the incident.

Ideally, this briefing will provide a fairly accurate picture of what resources are currently working the incident along with their incident location, what additional resources have been ordered, and whether any check-in locations have been established.

Use the checklist as a guide to ensure a thorough briefing.

☐ *Incident situation: magnitude and potential of the incident*

☐ *Command structure (single or unified)*

☐ *Resources currently working the incident and their assignment (e.g., Search Group)*

☐ *Any established check-in locations*

☐ *Operational period*

☐ *Agencies and jurisdictions involved*

☐ *Resources ordered*

☐ *Resource request process*

Make sure you request a copy of the ICS-201, Incident Briefing Form (pages 3 and 4) or other documents that can help you begin to develop an accurate resource "picture."

Determine the Resources Unit Staffing Needs

Experience is the best guide for determining staffing needs. However, the figure below provides a reference to help determine the number of personnel necessary to successfully manage all the responsibilities of the Resources Unit.

The number of check-in recorders is not fixed because it depends on the number of check-in locations established and the number of check-in recorders needed at each of those locations.

Resources Unit Staffing Guide
(per 12-hour period)

Resources Unit Position	Size of the Incident (Number of Divisions/Groups)				
	2	5	10	15	25
Resources Unit Leader	1	1	1	1	1
Status Recorders	1	2	3	3	3
Check-in Recorder	As needed				
Total Staffing	2	3	4	4	4

"Resources Unit Staffing Guide"

Check-in form (ICS-211)

The ICS-211, Check-in Form, is used to track personnel and equipment resources reporting to the incident.

ICS Check-in Form

CHECK-IN LIST (ICS-211)	1. INCIDENT NAME Meridian Flood	2. CHECK-IN LOCATION 4th Street Staging	3. DATE/TIME 11-15 1230

4. LIST OF PERSONNEL (OVERHEAD) BY AGENCY NAME- OR LIST OF EQUIPMENT BY THE FOLLOWING (see note below) *:
S=Supplies   H=Helicopter
O=Overhead   C=Crew
E=Equipment   D=Dozer
A=Aircraft   VL=Vessel
* If the resource does not fit one of the above categories, make sure that whatever abbreviation is used is documented and used consistently throughout the response (e.g., VL=Vessel)

CHECK-IN INFORMATION

AGENCY	ST/TF	KIND	TYPE	RESOURCE IDENTIFIER	5. ORDER/ NUMBER	6. DATE/TIME CHECK-IN	7. LEADER'S NAME	8. TOTAL NO. PERSONNEL	9. INCIDENT CONTACT INFORMATION	10. HOME UNIT	11. METHOD OF TRAVEL	12. INCIDENT ASSIGNMENT	13. OTHER QUALIFICATION	14. TIME SENT TO RESTAT
FRAM		C		MESA #3	C-008	11/15 1230	B. RIGGS	21	555-2310	SPRINGS	BUS	SEARCH GROUP		1330
BFD		O		P. Robert	O-020	11/15 1305		1	555-0909	ARCATA	AIR	DIVS	Staging Manager	1330
USCG		VL		44120	VL-023	11/15 1310	KAMMER	4		EUREKA		SEARCH GROUP		1330
PHL		E	2	AMBULANCE #1	E-025	11/15 1315	S. MILLER	2	555-3891	ARCATA		SEARCH GROUP		1330

"ICS-211 Check-in form"

Check-in of resources includes recording of the following (see sample ICS-211 Check-in form):

- Agency: This is the agency from where the resource came.

- ST/TF: In this block of the ICS-211, you want to note whether the resource that is checking in is a Strike Team (ST) or a Task Force (TF). For example, for a Strike Team place ST in the block.

- Resource Identifier: This is the unique identifier of the resource that distinguishes it from other resources. For example, the crew in the sample ICS-211 Check-in form is called the MESA #3 crew. If the resource is a person, then the name is recorded as shown in the sample ICS-211 with P. Robert.

- Kind: Is the resource a crew (C); vessel (VL); equipment (E); etc.? There are many kinds of resources.

- Type: If the resource checking into the incident is typed, record that information in this block. You can see in the sample ICS-211 where the Check-In Recorder placed the number "2" next to the resource identified as Ambulance 1.

- Order Request Number: When resources are requested, they should receive an order request number. Currently, outside the wildland fire discipline this is not a well-developed system, however, the National Incident Management System recognizes the value of using a resource order number to track resources.

- Date/Time Check-in: This is the date and time that the resource (personnel or equipment) arrives on-scene at the incident and checks in.

- Leader's Name: This is the name of the person that's in charge of the resource; e.g., leader of a 20-person crew or the pilot-in-charge of a helicopter.

- Total Number of Personnel: This is where the number of personnel who come with a resource is recorded; for example, 4 personnel attached to a fire engine or 2 personnel attached to a law enforcement vehicle.

- Incident Contact Information: This is where you can record the cell phone number that can be given to the Communications Unit Leader.

- Home Unit: This is the city or town where the resource is permanently assigned.

- Method of Travel: This is how the resource arrived at the incident; for example, bus, government vehicle, airplane.

- Incident Assignment: This is the initial assignment of the resource when ordered to the incident.

- Other Qualifications: This is where other ICS qualifications are recorded. For example, a Planning Section Chief may also be qualified as an Operations Section Chief.

- Sent to Resource Status Recorder (RESTAT): This is the time when the Check-in Recorder sends the check-in information to the Resources Unit.

Determine Resources Already in the Field
(field verification)

Establishing check-in enables the Resources Unit Leader to record all resources arriving on-scene, but how about the resources that were already working the incident before check-in was established?

It's vital that the RESL verify the resources (equipment and personnel) and location of those resources that arrived on-scene prior to the establishment of check-in.

To do this, the RESL should conduct field verification. This can be done in several ways:

- Use Field Observers to get the information
- Send Check-in Recorders when available
- Debrief Supervisors coming off-shift

However it gets done, field verification combined with an effective check-in process will give the Resources Unit Leader confidence in the kind, type, numbers, and location of incident resources. Verification should also include nonoperational resources such as the Supply Unit Leader.

T-Card System (tracking incident resources)

T-cards are a visual method to track the location and status of resources. There are seven color-coded T-cards to track the most common incident resources. Helicopter, aircraft, personnel, and the miscellaneous T-cards are generic to all incidents and can be used regardless of the type of incident. Dozers, engines, and crew T-cards are not as versatile, but can still be used for a non-wildland fire incident.

If a particular T-card does not fit neatly into your emergency response, you only have to provide a legend so that everyone understands which cards represent which kind of resource.

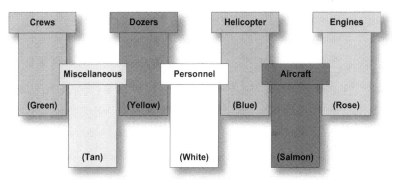

"There are seven color-coded T-cards to track incident resources"

Filling out the T-cards

Regardless of the color of the T-card, the information that is placed on them primarily comes from the ICS-211, Check-in form. The layout of each card may differ from the example on the opposite page, but the differences are minimal.

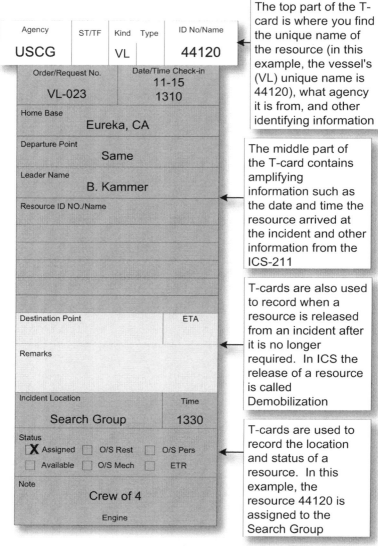

Agency	ST/TF	Kind	Type	ID No/Name
USCG		**VL**		**44120**

Order/Request No.	Date/Time Check-in
VL-023	**11-15** **1310**

Home Base
> Eureka, CA

Departure Point
> Same

Leader Name
> B. Kammer

Resource ID NO./Name

Destination Point	ETA

Remarks

Incident Location	Time
Search Group	**1330**

Status
- **X** Assigned ☐ O/S Rest ☐ O/S Pers
- ☐ Available ☐ O/S Mech ☐ ETR

Note
> Crew of 4

> Engine

The top part of the T-card is where you find the unique name of the resource (in this example, the vessel's (VL) unique name is 44120), what agency it is from, and other identifying information

The middle part of the T-card contains amplifying information such as the date and time the resource arrived at the incident and other information from the ICS-211

T-cards are also used to record when a resource is released from an incident after it is no longer required. In ICS the release of a resource is called Demobilization

T-cards are used to record the location and status of a resource. In this example, the resource 44120 is assigned to the Search Group

"Front side of the rose-color T-card"

16-11

Every time the status of a resource (Assigned, Available, and Out-of-Service) or its location (Division A, Search Group, etc.) is changed, that change is reflected on the T-card.

If the Resources Unit Leader is doing his or her job correctly, a properly maintained T-card will have both the current status and location of the resource as well as a historical record.

To avoid confusion, a line is drawn through historical resource status information. On the opposite page is the backside of the rose-color T-card with both historical information and current information.

Agency	ST/TF	Kind	Type	ID No/Name
USCG		VL		44120

Incident Location	Time
Bayfield Marina	1820

Status
☐ Assigned ☐ O/S Rest ☐ O/S Pers
☐ Available ☒ O/S Mech ☐ ETR

Note Vessel experiencing engine problems

Incident Location	Time
Search Group	1940

Status
☒ Assigned ☐ O/S Rest ☐ O/S Pers
☐ Available ☐ O/S Mech ☐ ETR

Note Repairs made -- vessel returned to Search Group

Incident Location	Time

Status
☐ Assigned ☐ O/S Rest ☐ O/S Pers
☐ Available ☐ O/S Mech ☐ ETR
Note

Incident Location	Time

Status
☐ Assigned ☐ O/S Rest ☐ O/S Pers
☐ Available ☐ O/S Mech ☐ ETR
Note

Here the 44120 was placed out-of-service due to mechanical problems (O/S Mech)

A new "incident location" block on the T-card should be used each time a change in the status or assignment occurs. Once repairs were made, the 44120 was again assigned to the Search Group.

The Resources Unit must be notified of all resource status changes or it will not have timely, accurate information.

"On the back side of the rose-color T-card you can record the change in a resource's status or location up to four times before you have to begin with a new card"

The white-color T-card is used to track overhead personnel. Overhead are those responders in management positions such as the Operations Section Chief and those in direct support of management activities such as Check-in Recorders.

The white-color T-card also has a place to note other ICS qualifications (e.g., Staging Area Manager) that an individual might carry. Knowing other ICS qualifications enables the RESL to have more flexibility in assigning the individual on the incident.

Agency	Name	Incident Assignment
BFD	P. Robert	DIVS

Order/Request No.	Date/Time Check-in
O-020	11-15 1310

Home Base

Arcata, CA

Departure Point

Butte

Method of Travel

☐ Own ☐ Bus ☐ Air

Other

Gov Sedan

On Manifest	Weight
☐ Yes ☒ No	

Date/Time Ordered	ETA

Destination Point

Remarks (include other qualifications)

Staging Area Manager

Incident Location	Time
Search Group	1330

Status

☒ Assigned ☐ O/S Rest ☐ O/S Pers

☐ Available ☐ O/S Mech ☐ ETR

Note

Contact # 555-0909

Personnel

The white T-card (personnel) contains a place to track other ICS qualifications

"The white-color T-card tracks personnel"

Below is the back side of the white-color T-card showing both current and historical information on a resource's status and location.

Agency	Name	Incident Assignment
BFD	**P. Robert**	**DIVS**

Incident Location	Time
Incident Camp	11-15 2030

Status
- [ ] Assigned
- [X] O/S Rest
- [ ] O/S Pers
- [ ] Available
- [ ] O/S Mech
- [ ] ETR
- Not e

As soon as P. Robert's new status and location is recorded the old information has a line drawn across it

Incident Location	Time
Search Group	11-16 0500

Status
- [X] Assigned
- [ ] O/S Rest
- [ ] O/S Pers
- [ ] Available
- [ ] O/S Mech
- [ ] ETR

Note

This is P. Robert's current assignment as of 0500 on 16 November. P. Robert is again assigned to the Search Group

Incident Location	Time

Status
- [ ] Assigned
- [ ] O/S Rest
- [ ] O/S Pers
- [ ] Available
- [ ] O/S Mech
- [ ] ETR

Note

Incident Location	Time

Status
- [ ] Assigned
- [ ] O/S Rest
- [ ] O/S Pers
- [ ] Available
- [ ] O/S Mech
- [ ] ETR

Note

"Back of the white-color T-card"

Establishing a Resources Status Display Using T-Cards

Once the T-card is filled out, it's placed in the Resources Status Display that shows its location on the incident.

Incident locations are recorded on gray-color cards called Header T-cards or Label T-cards. The naming on Header T-cards can come from a few sources. The Operations Section Chief (OSC) determines how an incident is divided up operationally (e.g., Division A, Search Group). As the RESL, simply follow the naming convention provided by the OSC and fill in the Header cards accordingly.

To track overhead personnel in the Incident Command Post the RESL determines how best to display the information, this is a second source for the naming that appears on the Header cards. For example, you might label a Header card Command, and place the Incident Commander(s), Liaison Officer, Safety Officer, and Public Information Officers cards under it. For those working in the Planning Section, you may label a Header card Planning and place all overhead personnel in Planning under that card.

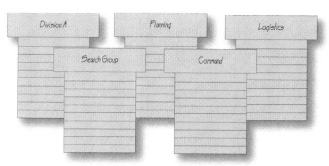

"Header T-cards"

Resource Assignment Flowchart During an Operational Period

The flowchart below outlines the process that the OSC follows to fill unanticipated resource requirements.

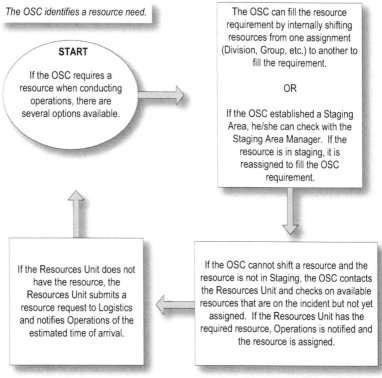

The OSC identifies a resource need.

START

If the OSC requires a resource when conducting operations, there are several options available.

The OSC can fill the resource requirement by internally shifting resources from one assignment (Division, Group, etc.) to another to fill the requirement.

OR

If the OSC established a Staging Area, he/she can check with the Staging Area Manager. If the resource is in staging, it is reassigned to fill the OSC requirement.

If the OSC cannot shift a resource and the resource is not in Staging, the OSC contacts the Resources Unit and checks on available resources that are on the incident but not yet assigned. If the Resources Unit has the required resource, Operations is notified and the resource is assigned.

If the Resources Unit does not have the resource, the Resources Unit submits a resource request to Logistics and notifies Operations of the estimated time of arrival.

"Resource assignment flowchart during an operational period"

RESL Support to the Tactics Meeting

Once the OSC has determined the work assignment and resources, he or she will list the number of each resource required. In this example the OSC requires 1 ambulance, 1 helicopter, 1 rescue boat, and 1 search team to accomplish the work assigned to the Search Group.

The REQ block on the ICS-215

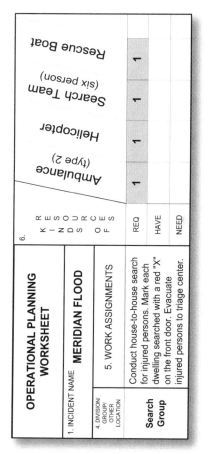

"REQ block on the ICS-215 form"

Once the OSC has laid out the resource requirements for the next operational period, you, as the Resources Unit Leader, will fill in the HAVE block of the ICS-215. The HAVE block contains the number and kind of tactical resources available for the next operational period.

The HAVE block on the ICS-215

OPERATIONAL PLANNING WORKSHEET		RESOURCES	Ambulance (type 2)	Helicopter	Search Team (six person)	Rescue Boat
1. INCIDENT NAME **MERIDIAN FLOOD**	5. WORK ASSIGNMENTS	REQ	1	1	1	1
		HAVE	1	0	1	1
4. DIVISION/ GROUP/ OTHER LOCATION		NEED				
Search Group	Conduct house-to-house search for injured persons. Mark each dwelling searched with a red "X" on the front door. Evacuate injured persons to triage center.					

"HAVE block on the ICS-215 form"

Once the REQ and HAVE blocks have been filled in it is easy to determine which resources need to be ordered and in what quantities.

The NEED block on the ICS-215

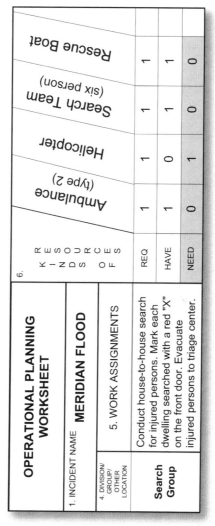

OPERATIONAL PLANNING WORKSHEET		Ambulance (type 2)	Helicopter	Search Team (six person)	Rescue Boat
1. INCIDENT NAME **MERIDIAN FLOOD**					
4. DIVISION/ GROUP/ OTHER LOCATION	5. WORK ASSIGNMENTS	6. RESOURCES OF			
Search Group	Conduct house-to-house search for injured persons. Mark each dwelling searched with a red "X" on the front door. Evacuate injured persons to triage center.	REQ			
		1	1	1	1
	HAVE	1	0	1	1
	NEED	0	1	0	0

"NEED block on the ICS-215 form"

The ICS-204 Assignment List

To complete the ICS-204, Assignment List the RESL works with the Operations Section Chief, Safety Officer, and Communications Unit Leader.

1. BRANCH	2. ~~DIVISION~~/GROUP Search	ASSIGNMENT LIST			
3. INCIDENT NAME **MERIDIAN FLOOD**		4. OPERATIONAL PERIOD (Date and Time) 16 Nov 0600 to 16 Nov 1800			

5. OPERATIONS PERSONNEL

OPERATIONS CHIEF_____ L. Hewett _____ ~~DIVISION~~/GROUP SUPERVISOR_____ P. Robert _____

BRANCH DIRECTOR_____ AIR TACTICAL GROUP SUPERVISOR_____

6. RESOURCES ASSIGNED THIS PERIOD

STRIKE TEAM/TASK FORCE RESOURCE DESIGNATOR	EMT	LEADER	NUMBER PERSONS	TRANS NEEDED	DROP OFF POINT/TIME	PICK UP POINT/TIME
MESA #3		B. Riggs	21		0530	
44120		V. Kammer	4		0530	
Ambulance #1		S. Miller	2		0530	
Helicopter 12		T. Troutman	2			

7. ASSIGNMENT

Conduct house-to-house search for injured persons. Mark each dwelling searched with a red "X" on the front door. Evacuate injured persons to triage center.

8. SPECIAL INSTRUCTIONS

Work in teams of two or more at all times. Snakes are suspected to be in the work area, wear snake gators. Personal floatation devices should be worn. Daylight operations only. Conduct regular communications checks. Send hourly updates on the group's progress to the Situation Unit.

9. DIVISION/GROUP COMMUNICATIONS SUMMARY

FUNCTION		FREQ.	SYSTEM	CHAN.	FUNCTION		FREQ.	SYSTEM	CHAN.
COMMAND	LOCAL	CDF 1	King	1	SUPPORT	LOCAL			
	REPEAT					REPEAT			
DIV./GROUP TACTICAL		157.4505	King	3	GROUND TO AIR				

PREPARED BY (RESOURCES UNIT LEADER) A. Worth	APPROVED BY (PLANNING SECT. CH.) J. Gafkjen	DATE 16 Nov	TIME 0400

"The RESL is responsible for ensuring that the ICS-204s are correctly filled in"

The ICS-203 Organization Assignment List

The ICS-203 serves as a master list of names of personnel who are filling key incident command positions in the Command and General Staff, Unit Leaders in all of the sections, and the supervisory personnel in the Operations Section.

ORGANIZATION ASSIGNMENT LIST		Food Unit	
		Medical Unit	
1. Incident Name **MERIDIAN FLOOD**			
2. Date	3. Time		
		9. Operations Section	
4. Operational Period		Chief	
		Deputy	
Position	**Name**	Staging	
5. Incident Commander and Staff		Staging	
Incident Commander		Staging	
Deputy		**a. Branch I - Divisions/Groups**	
Safety Officer		Branch Director	
Information Officer		Deputy	
Liaison Officer		**Search** Group	P. Robert
Intelligence Officer		Division/Group	
6. Agency Representatives		Division/Group	
		b. Branch II - Divisions/Groups	
		Branch Director	
		Deputy	
		Division/Group	
7. Planning Section		Division/Group	
Chief		Division/Group	
Deputy		**c. Branch III - Divisions/Groups**	
Resources Unit		Branch Director	
Situation Unit		Deputy	
Documentation Unit		Division/Group	
Demobilization Unit		Division/Group	
Technical Specialists		Division/Group	
Human Resources		**d. Air Operations Branch**	
Training		Air Ops Branch Director	
		Air Attack Supervisor	
		Air Support Supervisor	
8. Logistics Section		Helicopter Coordinator	
Chief		Air Tanker Coordinator	
Deputy		**10. Finance Section**	
Supply Unit		Chief	
Facilities Unit		Deputy	
Ground Support Unit		Time Unit	
Communications Unit		Procurement Unit	
ICS-203	Prepared by Resources Unit		

"The ICS-203 is filled out using information from the Resources Status Display"

Resources Unit Leader Involvement in Demobilization

Demobilization is an orderly and planned process and the Resources Unit Leader has an important role in ensuring that the process is smooth.

Resources that are scheduled for demobilization are placed under a Header T-card labeled DEMOB. The tracking of resources does not end until the resource has physically departed the incident and is en route to its home (parent) unit or off to another incident.

Once the Demobilization Unit Leader has advised the RESL that the resource is released, the T-card is updated with the demobilization information and then it's sent to the Documentation Unit Leader as part of the incident's historical record.

The RESL should always be looking for resources that are checked into the incident but have not been used for several operational periods and discuss demobilizing the resource with the Planning and Operations Section Chiefs.

LOGISTICS SECTION

"Logistics Section organization"

Logistics Section Chief (LSC)

The LSC is responsible for providing facilities, services, and material in support of the incident. The LSC participates in the development and implementation of the IAP and activates and supervises the Branches and Units within the Logistics Section.

The LSC may have deputies who may be from the same agency or from an assisting agency. The Deputy LSC must have the same qualifications as the person for whom they work, as they must be ready to take over that position at any time.

The major responsibilities of the LSC are:

 a. Review Common Responsibilities in Chapter 2

 b. Plan the organization of the Logistics Section

 c. Assign work locations and preliminary work tasks to Section personnel

 d. Notify the Resources Unit of the Logistics Section Units activated, including names and locations of assigned personnel

 e. Assemble and brief Logistics Branch Directors and Unit Leaders

 f. Determine and supply immediate incident resource and facility needs

 g. In conjunction with Command, develop and advise all Sections of the resource approval and request process

 h. Review proposed tactics for upcoming operational period for ability to provide resources and logistical support

i. Identify long-term service and support requirements for planned and expected operations

j. Advise Command and other Section Chiefs on resource availability to support incident needs

k. Review and provide input into the Communications Plan, Medical Plan and Traffic Plan

l. Identify resource needs for incident contingencies

m. Coordinate and process requests for additional resources

n. Track resource effectiveness and make necessary adjustments

o. Advise the IMT on current service and support capabilities

p. Request and/or set up expanded ordering processes as appropriate to support incident

q. Develop recommended list of Section resources to be demobilized and initiate recommendation for release when appropriate

r. Receive and implement applicable portions of the incident Demobilization Plan

s. Ensure the general welfare and safety of Logistics Section personnel

t. Maintain Unit Log (ICS-214)

Service Branch

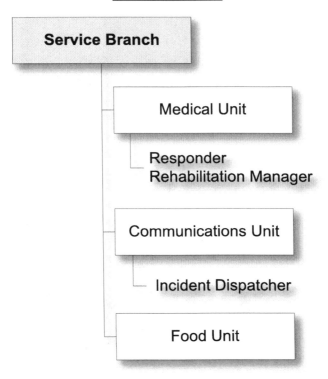

Service Branch

Medical Unit

Responder
Rehabilitation Manager

Communications Unit

Incident Dispatcher

Food Unit

"Service Branch organization"

Service Branch Director (SVBD)

The SVBD, when activated, is under the supervision of the LSC and is responsible for the management of all service activities at the incident. The Branch Director supervises the operations of the Communications, Medical and Food Units.

The major responsibilities of the SVBD are:

a. Review Common Responsibilities in Chapter 2

b. Obtain working materials

c. Determine the level of service required to support operations

d. Confirm dispatch of Branch personnel

e. Participate in planning meetings of Logistics Section personnel

f. Review the IAP

g. Organize and prepare assignments for Service Branch personnel

h. Coordinate activities of Branch Units

i. Inform the LSC of Branch activities

j. Resolve Service Branch problems

k. Maintain Unit Log (ICS-214)

Medical Unit Leader (MEDL)

The MEDL, under the direction of the Service Branch Director or Logistics Section Chief, is primarily responsible for the development of the Medical Plan; providing medical care and overseeing the health aspects of response personnel; obtaining medical aid and transportation for injured and ill response personnel; coordinating with other functions to resolve health and safety issues; and preparation of medical reports and records.

The major responsibilities of the MEDL are:

a. Review Common Responsibilities in Chapter 2

b. Review Unit Leader Responsibilities in Chapter 2

c. Participate in Logistics Section/Service Branch planning activities

d. Establish the Medical Unit

e. Prepare the Medical Plan (ICS-206)

f. Provide any relevant medical input into the planning process for strategy development

g. Coordinate with Safety Officer, Operations, hazmat specialists, and others on proper personnel protection procedures for incident personnel

h. Prepare procedures for major medical emergencies

i. Develop transportation routes and methods for injured incident personnel

j. Ensure incident personnel patients are tracked as they move from origin, care facility and disposition

k. Provide continuity of medical care for incident personnel

l. Declare major medical emergency as appropriate

m. Provide or oversee medical and rehab care delivered to incident personnel

n. Monitor health aspects of incident personnel including excessive incident stress

o. Respond to requests for medical aid, medical transportation and medical supplies

p. In conjunction with Finance/Administration Section, prepare and submit necessary authorizations, reports and administrative documentation related to injuries, compensation or death of incident personnel

q. Coordinate personnel and mortuary affairs for incident personnel fatalities

r. Provide for security and proper disposition of incident medical records

s. Maintain Unit Log (ICS-214)

Responder Rehabilitation Manager (REHB)

The REHB reports to the Medical Unit Leader and is responsible for the rehabilitation of incident personnel who are suffering from the effects of strenuous work and/or extreme conditions.

The major responsibilities of the REHB are:

a. Review Common Responsibilities in Chapter 2

b. Designate the responder rehabilitation location and announce the location using the designation "Rehab"

c. Coordinate with MEDL to request necessary medical personnel to evaluate the medical condition of personnel being rehabilitated

d. Request necessary resources for rehabilitation of personnel, (e.g., water, juice, personnel)

e. Request food through the Food Unit or LSC, as necessary, for personnel being rehabilitated

f. Release rehabilitated personnel for reassignment

g. Maintain appropriate records and documentation

h. Maintain Unit Log (ICS-214)

Communications Unit Leader (COML)

The COML is responsible for developing plans for the effective use of incident communications equipment and facilities; installing and testing of communications equipment; supervision of Incident Communications Center; distribution of communications equipment to incident personnel; and maintenance and repair of communications equipment.

The major responsibilities of the COML are:

a. Review Common Responsibilities in Chapter 2

b. Review Unit Leader Responsibilities in Chapter 2

c. Determine Unit personnel needs

d. Prepare and implement the Incident Radio Communications Plan (ICS-205)

e. Ensure the Incident Communications Center and the Message Center are established

f. Establish appropriate communications distribution/ maintenance locations within the Base

g. Ensure communications systems are installed and tested

h. Ensure an equipment accountability system is established

i. Ensure personal portable radio equipment is distributed per Incident Radio Communications Plan

j. Provide technical information as required on:
   - Adequacy of communications systems currently in operation
   - Geographic limitation on communications systems
   - Equipment capabilities/limitations

- Amount and types of equipment available
- Anticipated problems in the use of communications equipment

k. Supervise Communications Unit activities

l. Maintain records on all communications equipment as appropriate

m. Ensure equipment is tested and repaired

n. Recover equipment from personnel being demobilized

o. Maintain Unit Log (ICS-214)

Incident Dispatcher (INCM)

The INCM is responsible for receiving and transmitting radio and telephone messages among and between personnel and to provide dispatch services at the incident.

The major responsibilities of the INCM are:

a. Review Common Responsibilities in Chapter 2

b. Ensure adequate staffing

c. Obtain and review the IAP to determine the incident organization and Incident Radio Communications Plan

d. Set up Incident Communications Center and check-out equipment

e. Request service on any inoperable or marginal equipment

f. Set-up Message Center location, as required

g. Receive and transmit messages within and external to the incident

h. Maintain files of ICS-210 and ICS-213

i. Maintain a record of unusual incident occurrences

j. Provide a briefing to relief personnel on:
    - Current activities
    - Equipment status
    - Any unusual communications situations

k. Turn in appropriate documents to the Communications Unit Leader

l. Demobilize the Incident Communications Center in accordance with the Incident Demobilization Plan

m. Maintain Unit Log (ICS-214)

Food Unit Leader (FDUL)

The FDUL is responsible for supplying the food needs for the entire incident, including all remote locations, (e.g., Staging Areas), as well as providing food for personnel unable to leave tactical field assignments

The major responsibilities of the FDUL are:

a. Review Common Responsibilities in Chapter 2

b. Review Unit Leader Responsibilities in Chapter 2

c. Determine food and water requirements

d. Determine the method of feeding to best fit each facility or situation

e. Obtain necessary equipment and supplies

f. Ensure that well-balanced menus are provided

g. Order sufficient food and potable water from the Supply Unit

h. Maintain an inventory of food and water

i. Maintain food service areas, ensuring that all appropriate health and safety measures are being followed

j. Supervise Food Unit personnel as appropriate

k. Maintain Unit Log (ICS-214)

Support Branch

"Support Branch organization"

Support Branch Director (SUBD)

The SUBD, when activated, is under the direction of the LSC, and is responsible for the development and implementation of logistics plans in support of the Incident Action Plan. The SUBD supervises the operations of the Supply, Facilities, and Ground Support Units.

The major responsibilities of the SUBD are:

a. Review Common Responsibilities in Chapter 2

b. Review Unit Leader Responsibilities in Chapter 2

c. Identify Support Branch personnel dispatched to the incident

d. Determine initial support operations in coordination with the LSC and SVBD

e. Prepare initial organization and assignments for support operations

f. Assemble and brief Support Branch personnel

g. Determine if assigned Branch resources are sufficient

h. Maintain surveillance of assigned Units work progress and inform the LSC of their activities

i. Resolve problems associated with requests from the Operations Section

j. Maintain Unit Log (ICS-214)

Facilities Unit Leader (FACL)

The FACL is primarily responsible for the set up, maintenance and demobilization of incident facilities, (e.g., Base, ICP, Staging Areas), as well as security services required to support incident operations.

The FACL provides sleeping and sanitation facilities for incident personnel and manages Base operations. Each facility is assigned a manager who reports to the FACL and is responsible for managing the operation of the facility.

The major responsibilities of the FACL are:

a. Review Common Responsibilities in Chapter 2

b. Review Unit Leader Responsibilities in Chapter 2

c. Obtain a briefing from the SUBD or the LSC

d. Receive and review a copy of the IAP

e. Participate in Logistics Section/Support Branch planning activities

f. In conjunction with the Finance/Administration Section, determine locations suitable for incident support facilities and obtain permission to use from property owners

g. Inspect facilities prior to occupation and document conditions and preexisting damage

h. Determine requirements for each facility, including the ICP

i. Prepare layouts of incident facilities

j. Notify Unit Leaders of facility layout

k. Activate incident facilities

l. Provide Facility Managers and personnel to operate facilities

m. Provide sleeping facilities

n. Provide security services

o. Provide food and water service

p. Provide sanitation and shower service, as needed

q. Provide facility maintenance services, (e.g., sanitation, lighting, clean up, trash removal)

r. Inspect all facilities for damage and potential claims

s. Demobilize incident facilities

t. Maintain facility records

u. Maintain Unit Log (ICS-214)

Security Manager (SECM)

The SECM is responsible for providing security to protect incident personnel and property from loss or damage.

The major responsibilities of the SECM are:

a. Review Common Responsibilities in Chapter 2

b. Establish contacts with local law enforcement agencies, as required

c. Request personnel to support work assignments

d. Ensure security of classified material and/or systems

e. Ensure that support personnel are qualified to manage security problems

f. Develop Security Plan for incident facilities

g. Adjust Security Plan for personnel and equipment changes and releases

h. Coordinate security activities with appropriate incident personnel

i. Keep the peace, prevent assaults and settle disputes through coordination with Agency Representatives

j. Prevent theft of all government and personal property

k. Document complaints and suspicious occurrences

l. Maintain Unit Log (ICS-214)

Base Manager (BCMG)

The BCMG is responsible for ensuring that appropriate sanitation, security and facility management services are conducted at the Base.

The major responsibilities of the BCMG are:

a. Review Common Responsibilities in Chapter 2

b. Determine personnel support requirements

c. Obtain necessary equipment and supplies

d. Ensure that all facilities and equipment are set up and properly functioning

e. Supervise the establishment of
   - Sanitation facilities (to include showers)
   - Sleeping facilities

f. Make sleeping area assignments

g. Adhere to all applicable safety and health standards and regulations

h. Ensure that facility maintenance services are provided

i. Maintain Unit Log (ICS-214)

Supply Unit Leader (SPUL)

The SPUL is primarily responsible for receiving, storing and distributing all supplies for the incident; maintaining an inventory of supplies; and storing, disbursing and servicing non-expendable supplies and equipment.

The major responsibilities of the SPUL are:

a. Review Common Responsibilities in Chapter 2

b. Review Unit Leader Responsibilities in Chapter 2

c. Participate in Logistics Section/Support Branch planning activities

d. Determine the type and amount of supplies enroute

e. Review the IAP for information on operations of the Supply Unit

f. Develop and implement safety and security requirements

g. Order, receive, distribute and store supplies and equipment

h. Receive and respond to requests for personnel, supplies and equipment

i. Maintain an inventory of supplies and equipment

j. Service reusable equipment

k. Submit reports to the SUBD

l. Maintain Unit Log (ICS-214)

Ordering Manager (ORDM)

The ORDM is responsible for placing all orders for supplies and equipment for the incident. The ORDM reports to the SPUL.

The major responsibilities of the ORDM are:

 a. Review Common Responsibilities in Chapter 2

 b. Obtain necessary agency(ies) order forms

 c. Establish ordering procedures

 d. Establish name and telephone numbers of agency(ies) personnel receiving orders

 e. Set up filing system

 f. Obtain roster of incident personnel who have ordering authority

 g. Obtain list of previously ordered supplies and equipment

 h. Ensure order forms are filled out correctly

 i. Place orders in a timely manner

 j. Consolidate orders, when possible

 k. Identify times and locations for delivery of supplies and equipment

 l. Keep Receiving and Distribution Manager (RCDM) informed of orders placed

 m. Submit all ordering documents to the Documentation Control Unit through the SPUL Leader before demobilization

 n. Maintain Unit Log (ICS-214)

Receiving and Distribution Manager (RCDM)

The RCDM is responsible for receiving and distributing all supplies and equipment (other than tactical resources) and the service and repair of tools and equipment. The RCDM reports to the SPUL.

The major responsibilities of the RCDM are:

a. Review Common Responsibilities in Chapter 2

b. Order required personnel to operate supply area

c. Organize the physical layout of the supply area

d. Establish procedures for operating the supply area

e. Set up a filing system for receiving and distributing supplies and equipment

f. Maintain inventory of supplies and equipment

g. Develop security requirement for supply area

h. Establish procedures for receiving supplies and equipment

i. Submit necessary reports to the SPUL

j. Notify ORDM of supplies and equipment received

k. Provide necessary supply records to SPUL

l. Maintain Unit Log (ICS-214)

Ground Support Unit Leader (GSUL)

The GSUL is primarily responsible for ensuring:

- Repair of primary tactical equipment, vehicles, mobile ground support equipment and fueling services

- Transportation of personnel, supplies, food and equipment in support of incident operations

- Recording all ground equipment usage time, including contract equipment assigned to the incident

- Implementing the Traffic Plan for the incident

The major responsibilities of the GSUL are:

a. Review Common Responsibilities in Chapter 2

b. Review Unit Leader Responsibilities in Chapter 2

c. Participate in Support Branch/Logistics Section planning activities

d. Develop and implement the Traffic Plan

e. Support out-of-service resources

f. Notify the Resources Unit of all status changes on support and transportation vehicles

g. Arrange for and activate fueling, maintenance and repair of ground resources

h. Maintain Support Vehicle Inventory and transportation vehicles (ICS-218)

i. Provide transportation services IAW requests from the LSC or SUBD

j. Collect use information on rented equipment

k. Requisition maintenance and repair supplies, (e.g., fuel, spare parts)

l. Maintain incident roads

m. Submit reports to SUBD as directed

n. Maintain Unit Log (ICS-214)

Equipment Manager (EQPM)

The EQPM provides:

- Service, repair and fuel for all incident vehicles, vessels and equipment
- Transportation and support vehicle services
- Records of equipment use and service provided

The major responsibilities of the EQPM are:

a. Review Common Responsibilities in Chapter 2

b. Obtain the IAP to determine locations for assigned resources, Staging Area locations and fueling and service requirements for all resources

c. Provide maintenance and fueling according to schedule

d. Prepare schedules to maximize use of available transportation

e. Provide transportation and support vehicles for incident use

f. Coordinate with Agency Representatives on service and repair policies, as required

g. Inspect equipment condition and ensure coverage by equipment agreement

h. Determine supplies (e.g., gasoline, diesel, oil and parts needed to maintain equipment in an efficient operating condition) and place orders with the Supply Unit

i. Maintain Support Vehicle Inventory (ICS-218)

j. Maintain equipment rental records

k. Maintain equipment service and use records

l. Check all service repair areas to ensure that all appropriate safety measures are being taken

m. Maintain Unit Log (ICS-214)

LOGISTICS SECTION CHIEF GUIDES

This Chapter is designed to help the Logistics Section Chief in carrying out his or her responsibilities.

✓ *Logistics Section Chief In-briefing Checklist*

✓ *Logistics Section Chief Staffing and Space Considerations Checklist*

✓ *Directions to the Facility Unit Leader (FACL)*

✓ *Relocating the Incident Command Post*

✓ *Directions to the Supply Unit Leader (SPUL)*

✓ *Directions to the Ground Support Unit Leader (GSUL)*

✓ *Directions to the Medical Unit Leader (MEDL)*

✓ *Directions to the Food Unit Leader (FDUL)*

✓ *Directions to the Communications Unit Leader (COML)*

✓ *LSC Role in the ICS Planning Process*

✓ *Incident Command Post Check-off Sheet*

Logistics Section Chief In-Briefing Checklist

If you're sent to an incident as the Logistics Section Chief, the Incident Commander/Unified Command (IC/UC) has recognized that the situation they're facing will require a dedicated and concentrated logistical effort to help bring the crisis under control. There's going to be a lot going on when you arrive so use the checklist below to ensure that you receive a thorough briefing.

- ☐ *Incident situation: magnitude and potential of the incident*
- ☐ *Information on current Logistics Section activities/ status*
- ☐ *Facilities already established*
- ☐ *Facilities that will be required (in priority order)*
- ☐ *Current incident organizational structure*
- ☐ *Expected incident duration*
- ☐ *Estimate on the potential size of the response organization*
- ☐ *Initial instructions concerning the tasks expected of the Logistics Section*
- ☐ *Command and General Staff priorities*
- ☐ *Operational period*
- ☐ *Clarify your ordering authority*
- ☐ *Determine if there are any concerns with:*
    - ☐ *Incident security*
    - ☐ *Facility safety*
    - ☐ *Medical support to responders*
    - ☐ *Communications*
- ☐ *Agencies and jurisdictions involved*

Logistics Section Chief's Staffing and Space Considerations Checklist

After you have received your briefing and have a better understanding of what you are up against, take some time to consider the staffing that you'll need to logistically support the incident and how much work space is needed for your logistics team.

- ☐ *In determining Section staffing, consider:*
    - ☐ *Functions that have to be accomplished (medical, food, communications center, etc.)*
    - ☐ *Length of the operational period*
    - ☐ *Required staffing (12/24 hour shifts)*
- ☐ *Identify any special requirements that the Section will need:*
    - ☐ *Equipment*
    - ☐ *Facilities*
    - ☐ *Labor*
- ☐ *Consider need for Support or Services Branch Directors*
- ☐ *Identify Logistics Section work space needs and assigned units*
    - ☐ *Accessible*
    - ☐ *Adequate*
    - ☐ *Proximity to Finance/Administration Section*
    - ☐ *Adaptable to computer/communications equipment*

Directions to the Facilities Unit Leader (FACL)

The pace of response operations and influx of personnel can quickly gobble up square footage. The Facilities Unit must have the facilities necessary to absorb the increase in personnel. The Facilities Unit is responsible for the layout, activation, and setup of incident facilities and the Facilities Unit Leader needs to understand the space requirements for each designated facility. Facilities may include: Incident Command Post, Base, and Camps.

- Conduct a facility needs assessment

- Ensure that the ICP is established to meet the needs of the incident

- Ensure that all incident facilities are environmentally and structurally sound, and are:
  - Located:
    - Upwind and uphill
    - In proximity to area of operations
    - With easy ingress and egress
  - Have adequate:
    - Security and parking
    - Sanitation facilities
    - Electrical power
    - Telephone and broadband capability
  - Clearly marked to enable responders to find them day and night

- If required, establish incident base

- Ensure that sanitation, rest and food facilities are established and maintained

- Provide for the maintenance of incident equipment resources

- Establish incident security for all established facilities

- Demobilize incident facilities as the incident winds down

Relocating the Incident Command Post (ICP)

If the incident requires a larger and more permanent Incident Command Post (ICP), the FACL will have to find an alternate location and develop a relocation plan that is acceptable to the IC/UC.

If you find yourself in a situation that requires shifting the ICP you can minimize the impact on operations by developing a relocation plan. The checklist below is a good guide for what the relocation plan should contain.

Relocation Checklist

Components of a relocation plan:

- Objectives for relocating the ICP
- Directions and map to the new ICP location
- Parking information
- Feeding routine
- Diagram of ICP showing location of all key ICS functions (e.g., Resources Unit)
- Facility security
- List of ICP phone numbers

Directions to the Supply Unit Leader (SPUL)

The Supply Unit has an enormous responsibility in ensuring that the response is successful. A mistake in ordering resources and supplies will ripple through the response effort. Take time to make sure that the Supply Unit Leader is well aware of your expectations.

- Ensure that the Supply Unit is staffed with the appropriate representatives from the primary responding agencies
- Develop an ordering process for the Logistics Section Chief's approval. Make sure the process includes:
  - List of who has ordering authority
  - Requirement for a tracking number to be attached to each ordered item
- Establish an inventory and accountability system for shipping and receiving
- Ensure that all requests for tactical resources are routed through the Resources Unit before acting on them
- Maintain a matrix or spreadsheet to track all resources that have been ordered
- Work closely with the Resources Unit and Procurement Unit
- Manage and inventory non-tactical equipment
- Ensure that all invoices are forwarded to the Finance/Administration Section for payment
- Ensure that personnel who requested items are notified in a timely manner of the equipment arrival
- Ensure that storage areas are established for:
  - General supplies and equipment
  - Fuel
  - Hazardous materials
- Maintain a Unit Log, ICS-214

Directions to the Ground Support Unit Leader (GSUL)

The Ground Support Unit Leader is responsible for all ground support and transportation of personnel, supplies, food and equipment as well as fueling, service and maintenance of vehicles on the incident and implementing an incident Traffic Plan.

- Work closely with the Facilities Unit Leader to identify and establish equipment service area(s). Services to include:
  - Fueling
  - Maintenance
  - Repair
- Ensure close coordination with Operations, Food Unit, and Supply Unit in providing timely transportation and delivery of:
  - Incident Personnel
  - Supplies
  - Food
  - Equipment
- Work with the Resources Unit Leader to maintain an accurate inventory of all ground support vehicles (e.g., buses)
- Maintain a Unit Log, ICS-214

Directions to the Medical Unit Leader (MEDL)

The number one incident objective for every response is to ensure the safety of response personnel. The Medical Unit has an important role to play in achieving that objective, and, in the event an injury does occur, it's the Medical Unit that must be ready to react to ensure that the injured responder receives rapid attention.

- Ensure that medical aid is in place and ready to meet the needs of the incident

- Ensure that transportation for injured responders is available and well coordinated

- Work closely with the Safety Officer as you develop the incident's evacuation and emergency plans

- Ensure that the Medical Unit has the personnel and equipment to provide for rehabilitation of responders who are suffering from the strenuous work and/ or environmental conditions (heat, cold, etc.). Rehabilitation measures should include:

  - Critical Incident Stress Management (CISM) activities
  - A sheltered location for rehabilitating responders where they can get rest, water, and food

- Ensure that the medical portion of the Incident Action Plan is completed on time:

  - Develop the Medical Plan, ICS-206

- Ensure that there are adequate medical supplies to respond to any anticipated need

- Maintain a Unit Log, ICS-214

Directions to the Food Unit Leader (FDUL)

Feeding responders can be a daunting task, and if neglected, can have a negative impact on the response. The delivery of food must be timed to ensure that the field responders are ready to go to work at the start of the operational period and are not unnecessarily delayed due to an unprepared Food Unit.

- Determine the best method for feeding responders

- Determine the amount of food and water needed and ensure that it's distributed to all incident facilities

- Ensure that adequate food supplies, such as potable water and nonperishable food items are ordered to support operations

- Put in place a food-monitoring program that will ensure that the food is maintained and served in accordance with proper food-handling practices

- Monitor food service provider for compliance with proper food-handling practices

- Ensure accountability for all food and water ordered

- Consider need to serve warm meals versus cold "box lunches," especially when response operations are conducted in cold-weather conditions

- Maintain a Unit Log, ICS-214

Directions to the Communications Unit Leader (COML)

It is the Communications Unit Leader's responsibility to develop and implement a communications plan that meets the requirements of the incident. This can be a very complex task.

- Conduct a communications assessment to determine what kinds of equipment (e.g., radios, mobile phones, computers, telephones) and support are needed for incident operations. Assessment should include:
    - Understanding the topographic features where the incident is located
    - Knowing where the incident is projected to move in the coming hours or days
    - Determining what the future plans are for the incident (e.g., growth in the organization)
    - Determining what communications facilities are in the area currently (e.g., cell towers, repeaters)
    - Knowing whether secure communications are required
- Ensure the communications portions of the Incident Action Plan are completed on time:
    - Develop the Communications Plan, ICS-205; monitor implementation
    - Review and provide input into the Assignment Lists, ICS-204s
- Work closely with the Operations Section Chief to ensure that his/her communications needs are being met
- Provide communication equipment to response personnel and maintain an accountability of equipment that is checked-out
- Maintain a Unit Log, ICS-214

LSC Role in the ICS Planning Process

As a key member of the command team, you'll be attending several scheduled meetings and briefings throughout each operational period. The meetings and briefings are designed to ensure that everyone is working toward the same goals and to provide opportunity to get clarification and direction from the IC/UC.

It's your responsibility to be on time and prepared to support the process. As the Logistics Section Chief, here is of what is expected of you when you attend these meetings and briefings.

Command and General Staff Meeting

Early on during each operational period the IC/UC will meet with their Command and General Staff to brief them collectively on how they see the response effort is going, discuss incident objectives, and provide direction.

This is a good opportunity to brief the IC/UC on logistical concerns and to get clarification on items that involve the Logistics Section. Some areas of discussion may include:

- Clarification on the type and location of support facilities that will be required to support operations

- Identifying logistical limitations that will impact response operations

- Pointing out any problems with internal resource ordering process that are causing unnecessary delays in getting resources to the incident

Preparing for the Tactics Meeting

One of the responsibilities of each member of the Command and General Staff and their subordinates that attend meetings is to be prepared to provide the information necessary to ensure that the objectives for each meeting and briefing are accomplished. Prepare for the Tactics Meeting by:

- Understanding what resources are currently ordered to the incident and when those resources are expected to arrive on-scene

- Being prepared to discuss the status of communications and facilities. You need to let the Operations Section Chief (OSC) know the status so that he/she can take advantage of any logistical support

- Evaluating the availability of resources in the local, and, if necessary, regional area (this information will help you support the OSC who will begin listing the resources that are required on the incident)

Tactics Meeting

This is perhaps the most critical meeting in the ICS Planning Process. The reason you're attending this meeting is to work with the OSC and Planning Section Chief (PSC) to ensure that the OSC's plan is logistically supportable. Your responsibilities as the LSC during the Tactics Meeting are to:

- Review the proposed tactics
- Identify resource needs and where the OSC wants the resources to report (e.g., Bayfield Street Staging Area)
- Discuss availability of needed resources
- Identify resource shortfalls
- Identify any resource support requirements

The OSC will conduct tactical planning using an ICS-215, Operational Planning Worksheet. Using this form, the OSC will identify the operations organization (Divisions, Groups, Staging Areas, Task Forces, etc.) that will be required for the next operational period, record the work assignments that each organizational element will need to accomplish, and list the resources that are required to carry out each work assignment.

It's this last item, the resource requirements, that is of particular interest to you. It will be your responsibility to locate any identified resources that are not already at the incident and get those resources to the incident in time for the next operational period.

Below is a cutaway section of the ICS-215 that has been completely filled in. As the LSC, you're interested in the NEED block because that is what you'll have to order and get to the incident in time.

OPERATIONAL PLANNING WORKSHEET		6. RESOURCES	Ambulance (type 2)	Helicopter	Search Team (six person)	Rescue Boat
1. INCIDENT NAME **MERIDIAN FLOOD**						
4. DIVISION/ GROUP/ OTHER LOCATION	5. WORK ASSIGNMENTS					
Search Group	Conduct house-to-house search for injured persons. Mark each dwelling searched with a red "X" on the front door. Evacuate injured persons to triage center.	REQ	1	1	1	1
		HAVE	1	0	1	1
		NEED	0	1	0	0

"Upper left corner of the ICS-215 Operational Planning Worksheet"

Preparing for the Planning Meeting

Once you step out of the Tactics Meeting you'll likely become extremely busy managing all kinds of logistical issues, but make sure you take the time to properly prepare for the Planning Meeting. Here are some things you need to accomplish before that meeting:

- Meet with the Supply Unit Leader to ensure that the resources identified in the NEED block of the ICS-215 during the Tactics Meeting are ordered

- Keep the OSC and PSC informed of any required resources that you're unable to get for the next operational period

  - Suggest to Operations any alternatives that may be available, such as a smaller crane if a large one cannot be obtained. (It's possible that Operations can use a less-capable resource to do the job, but that the job will take longer. Operations can present this alternative to the IC/UC and set the expectation that more time will be required to accomplish the objective)

Planning Meeting

You'll attend the Planning Meeting with the other members of the Command and General Staff and it's in this meeting that the IC/UC will give provisional approval of the tactical plan. The IC/UC is going to be looking for you to verify that the tactical plan is logistically supportable because they know that the OSC's plan is only as good as the resources behind it.

- Verify support for the tactical plan
- Confirm availability of required resources and that they will arrive in time to support the response during the next operational period
- Provide estimates of future service and support requirements

Incident Action Plan Preparation

The Logistics Section is responsible for important sections of the IAP and it's your responsibility to ensure that those sections are accurate and submitted to Planning on time. Specifically, Logistics develops the following parts of the IAP:

- Communications Plan, ICS-205 (completed by the Communications Unit Leader)
  - In addition, the Communications Unit Leader fills in the communications portion of the Assignment Lists, ICS-204s
- Medical Plan, ICS-206 (completed by the Medical Unit Leader)

Operations Briefing

A portion of the Operations Briefing is set aside for logistical issues, and it provides you with an opportunity to brief the responders on several issues to include:

- *Reviewing the Communications Plan*
- *Reviewing the Medical Plan*
- *Reviewing the Traffic Plan*
- *Discussing other logistical issues that may be of concern to the field personnel*

Execute Plan and Assess Progress

Once the Operations Briefing is completed, the field personnel will begin implementing their portion of the Incident Action Plan for the operational period. While they're engaged in the tactical operations, you should:

- *Meet with the Logistics Section personnel to go over any issues and discuss the section's performance*
- *Throughout the operational period monitor ongoing logistical support and make adjustments as necessary to deliver the best service possible*
- *Maintain close interaction with other members of the Command and General Staff*

Incident Command Post Check-off Sheet

The checklist (opposite) is provided to help you establish an Incident Command Post that provides the incident command team with a proper facility and equipment to perform their job.

The list contains information on ICP site selection, setup and operating requirements, and equipment requirements. The list is not all inclusive, but it will get you started in the right direction.

Site Selection Criteria

- *Determine organization size and the space requirements of each function*

- *Is the proposed Incident Command Post (ICP) facility in a secure area?*

- *Is it located in proximity to the Incident?*

- *Is location convenient for agency/organization executives to access?*

- *Is there adequate secure parking?*

- *Is there appropriate work space separation?*

- *Is there adequate meeting/briefing room space?*

- *Are there additional telephone lines available and will the facility accommodate them?*

- *Are you able to control public access?*

- *Is it near a helicopter (pad/landing zone)?*

- *Is it in a quiet area away from major distractions such as airports and railroads?*

- *Is it in close proximity to billeting and feeding facilities such as other agency operations centers and Emergency Operations Centers?*

- *Do you know the rental or lease cost of the facility?*

- *Is there adequate wall space for required displays?*

- *Is it located out of harm's way?*

- *Would it be able to accommodate the potential need for a separate Joint Information Center?*

- *Is there additional space available for co-locating the incident base?*

Setup and Operating Requirements

- Develop a sketch map of the facility

- Develop clear directions and a map along with reference points for location of the facility

- Establish a check-in desk with a check-in recorder and ICS-211 forms

- Assign work space and identify each functional area (Planning, Operations, Logistics, Finance/Administration, Incident/Unified Command, etc.)

- Ensure that the check-in recorder knows the location of all functional areas

- Provide security for the facility and the parking area

- Establish facility and services contract and agreement to include daily maintenance

- Procure required furniture, equipment, and supplies for the ICP

- Install communications system

- Conduct facility safety and security evaluation

- Develop and post an emergency evacuation plan and brief staff

- If necessary, augment sanitation facilities

- If necessary, negotiate facility use agreement

Equipment Requirements

- *Fax machines incoming and outgoing*

- *Professional-quality copy machine*

- *Video projector and projection screen*

- *Easels and flip charts*

- *Wall clocks*

- *Monitors/televisions with connections that are compatible with audiovisual equipment*

- *Computers and printers*

- *ICS position vests*

- *Maps and charts as needed*

- *Dry-erase boards*

- *T-card racks to support Resources Unit Leader (resource status)*

- *Administrative support kits for Planning Section Chief, Logistics Section Chief, and Finance/Admin Section Chief*

FINANCE/ADMINISTRATION SECTION

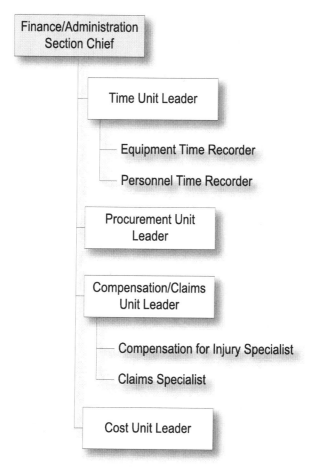

"Finance/Administration Section organization"

Finance/Administration Section Chief (FSC)

The FSC is responsible for all financial, administrative and cost analysis aspects of the incident and for supervising members of the Finance/Administration Section.

The FSC may have deputies, who may be from the same agency or from an assisting agency. The Deputy FSC must have the same qualifications as the person for whom they work, as they must be ready to take over that position at any time.

The major responsibilities of the FSC are:

a. Review Common Responsibilities in Chapter 2

b. Participate in incident planning meetings and briefings as required

c. Review operational plans and provide alternatives where financially appropriate

d. Manage all financial aspects of an incident

e. Provide financial and cost analysis information as requested

f. Gather pertinent information from briefings with responsible agencies

g. Develop an operating plan for the Finance/ Administration Section; fill supply and support needs

h. Determine the need to set up and operate an incident commissary

i. Meet with Assisting and Cooperating Agency Representatives, as needed

j. Maintain daily contact with agencies administrative headquarters on finance/administration matters

k. Ensure that all personnel time records are accurately completed and transmitted to home agencies, according to policy

l. Provide financial input to demobilization planning

m. Ensure that all obligation documents initiated at the incident are properly prepared and completed

n. Brief agency administrative personnel on all incident-related financial issues needing attention or follow-up prior to leaving incident

o. Develop recommended list of Section resources to be demobilized

p. Receive and implement applicable portions of the incident Demobilization Plan

q. Maintain Unit Log (ICS-214)

Time Unit Leader (TIME)

The TIME is responsible for equipment and personnel time recording and for managing the commissary operations.

The major responsibilities of the TIME are:

a. Review Common Responsibilities in Chapter 2

b. Review Unit Leader Responsibilities in Chapter 2

c. Determine incident requirements for the time recording function

d. Ensure that daily personnel time recording documents are prepared and in compliance with agency(ies) policy

e. Establish Time Unit objectives

f. Maintain separate logs for overtime hours

g. Establish commissary operation on larger or long-term incidents, as needed

h. Submit cost estimate data forms to the Cost Unit, as required

i. Maintain security of time records

j. Ensure that all records are current and complete prior to demobilization

k. Release time reports for assisting agency personnel to their respective Agency Representatives prior to demobilization

l. Brief the FSC on current problems, outstanding issues and follow-up requirements

m. Maintain Unit Log (ICS-214)

Equipment Time Recorder (EQTR)

Under supervision of the TIME, the EQTR is responsible for recording operating time for all equipment assigned to an incident.

The major responsibilities of the EQTR are:

a. Review Common Responsibilities in Chapter 2

b. Set up the EQTR function in location designated by the Time Unit Leader

c. Advise Ground Support Unit, Facilities Unit and Air Support Group of the requirement to establish and maintain a file for maintaining a daily record of equipment time

d. Assist Units in establishing a system for collecting equipment time reports

e. Post all equipment time tickets within 4 hours after the end of each operational period

f. Prepare a use and summary invoice for equipment, as required, within 12 hours after equipment arrival at the incident

g. Submit data to TIME for cost effectiveness analysis

h. Maintain current posting of all charges or credits for fuel, parts and services

i. Verify all time data and deductions with owner/ operator of equipment

j. Complete all forms according to agency specifications

k. Closeout forms prior to demobilization

l. Distribute copies per agency and incident policy

m. Maintain Unit Log (ICS-214)

Personnel Time Recorder (PTRC)

Under supervision of the TIME, the PTRC is responsible for overseeing the recording of time for all personnel assigned to an incident.

The major responsibilities of the PTRC are:

   a. Review Common Responsibilities in Chapter 2

   b. Establish and maintain a file for incident personnel time reports within the first operational period

   c. Initiate, gather or update a time report for all applicable personnel assigned to the incident for each operational period

   d. Ensure that all employee identification information is verified to be correct on the time report

   e. Post personnel travel and work hours, transfers, promotions, specific pay provisions and terminations to personnel time documents

   f.   Ensure that time reports are signed

   g. Close-out time documents prior to personnel leaving the incident

   h. Distribute all time documents according to agency policy

   i.   Maintain a log of excessive hours worked and give to the TIME daily

   j.   Maintain Unit Log (ICS-214)

Procurement Unit Leader (PROC)

The PROC is responsible for administering all financial matters pertaining to vendor contracts, leases and fiscal agreements.

The major responsibilities of the PROC are:

a. Review Common Responsibilities in Chapter 2

b. Review Unit Leader Responsibilities in Chapter 2

c. Review incident needs and any special procedures with Unit Leaders, as needed

d. Coordinate with local jurisdiction on plans and supply sources

e. Coordinate with FSC/LSC to obtain incident procurement plan

f. Prepare and authorize contracts, building and land-use agreements

g. Draft memoranda of understanding as necessary

h. Establish contracts and agreements with vendors

i. Provide for coordination between the Logistics Ordering Manager and all other procurement organizations supporting the incident

j. Ensure that a system is in place that meets agency property management requirements Ensure proper accounting for all new property

k. Interpret contracts and agreements; resolve disputes within delegated authority

l. Coordinate with the Compensation/Claims Unit for processing claims

m. Complete final processing of contracts and send documents for payment

n. Coordinate cost data in contracts with the COST

o. Brief the FSC on current problems, outstanding issues and follow-up requirements

p. Maintain Unit Log (ICS-214)

Compensation/Claims Unit Leader (COMP)

The COMP is responsible for the overall management and direction of all administrative matters pertaining to compensation for injury- and claims- related activities for an incident.

The major responsibilities of the COMP are:

a. Review Common Responsibilities in Chapter 2

b. Review Unit Leader Responsibilities in Chapter 2

c. Obtain a briefing from the FSC

d. Establish contact with the incident MEDL, SOF and LOFR (or Agency Representatives if no LOFR is assigned)

e. Determine the need for Compensation for Injury and Claims Specialists and order personnel as needed

f. Establish a Compensation for Injury work area within or as close as possible to the Medical Unit

g. Review Incident Medical Plan (ICS-206)

h. Ensure that the Claims Specialists (CLMS) have adequate workspace and supplies

i. Review and coordinate procedures for handling claims with the Procurement Unit

j. Brief the CLMS on incident activity

k. Periodically review logs and forms produced by the CLMS to ensure that they are complete, entries are timely and accurate, and that they are in compliance with agency requirements and policies

l. Ensure that all Compensation for Injury and Claims logs and forms are complete and routed to the appropriate agency for post-incident processing prior to demobilization

m. Keep the FSC briefed on unit status and activity

n. Demobilize unit in accordance with the Incident Demobilization Plan

o. Maintain Unit Log (ICS-214)

Compensation for Injury Specialist (INJR)

Under the supervision of the COMP, the Compensation for Injury Specialist is responsible for administering financial matters resulting from serious injuries and fatalities occurring on an incident. Close coordination is required with the Medical Unit.

The major responsibilities of the INJR are:

a. Review Common Responsibilities in Chapter 2

b. Collocate Compensation for Injury Specialist with the Medical Unit when possible

c. Establish procedure with Medical Unit Leader on prompt notification of injuries or fatalities

d. Obtain a copy of Medical Plan (ICS-206)

e. Provide written authority for persons requiring medical treatment

f. Ensure that correct agency forms are being used

g. Provide correct billing forms for transmittal to doctor and/or hospital

h. Coordinate with MEDL to keep informed on status of injured and/or hospitalized personnel

i. Obtain all witness statements from Safety Officer (SOF) and/or MEDL and review for completeness

j. Maintain a log of all injuries occurring at the incident

k. Coordinate/handle all administrative paperwork on serious injuries or fatalities

l. Coordinate with appropriate agencies to assume responsibility for injured personnel in local hospitals after demobilization

m. Maintain Unit Log (ICS-214)

Claims Specialist (CLMS)

Under the supervision of the COMP, the CLMS is responsible for managing all claims-related activities (other than injuries) for an incident.

The major responsibilities of the CLMS are:

a. Review Common Responsibilities in Chapter 2

b. Develop and maintain a log of potential claims

c. Coordinate a claims prevention plan with applicable incident functions

d. Initiate an investigation of all claims other than personnel injury

e. Ensure that property involved in an investigation is protected

f. Coordinate with the investigation team as necessary

g. Obtain witness statements pertaining to claims other than personnel injury

h. Document any incomplete investigations

i. Document follow-up actions for the local agency

j. Keep the COMP advised on the nature and status of all existing and potential claims

k. Ensure the use of correct agency forms

l. Maintain Unit Log (ICS-214)

Cost Unit Leader (COST)

The COST is responsible for collecting all cost data, performing cost effectiveness analyses and providing cost estimates and cost saving recommendations for the incident.

The major responsibilities of the COST are:

    a. Review Common Responsibilities in Chapter 2

    b. Review Unit Leader Responsibilities in Chapter 2

    c. Obtain a briefing from the FSC

    d. Coordinate with agency headquarters on cost reporting procedures

    e. Collect and record all cost data

    f. Develop incident cost summaries

    g. Prepare resources-use cost estimates for the Planning Section

    h. Make cost-saving recommendations to the FSC

    i. Ensure all cost documents are accurately prepared

    j. Maintain cumulative incident cost records

    k. Complete all records prior to demobilization

    l. Provide reports to the FSC

    m. Maintain Unit Log (ICS-214)

FINANCE/ADMINISTRATION SECTION CHIEF GUIDES

This Chapter is designed to help the FSC establish his or her section.

✓ *Finance/Administration Section Chief (FSC) In-briefing Checklist*

✓ *Directions to the Time Unit Leader*

✓ *Directions to the Procurement Unit Leader*

✓ *Directions to the Compensation/Claims Unit leader*

✓ *Directions to the Cost Unit Leader*

✓ *FSC Role in the ICS Planning Process*

Finance/Administration Section Chief In-briefing Checklist

The checklist below is a good guide to use when you are receiving your initial in-briefing.

- Incident situation: magnitude and potential of the incident

- Information on current Finance/Administration Section activities/status

- Fiscal limitations or constraints

- Established incident support facilities

- Status of any claims

- Agencies and private sector organizations that are on the incident

- Funding source(s)

- Current incident organizational structure

- Expected incident duration

- Estimate on the potential size of the response organization

- Initial instructions concerning the tasks expected of the Finance/Administration Section

- Command and General Staff priorities, limitations, and constraints and incident objectives

- Operational period

- Any accidents or injuries

- What has been purchased and how was it procured (e.g., procurement mechanism)

- Determine if there are any concerns with:
  - Funding
  - Contracts
  - Personnel and equipment time accounting

Directions to the Time Unit Leader (TIME)

Without an accurate tracking of personnel and equipment time on an incident, the cost of the response cannot be computed with any confidence and individual responders may not be compensated for their efforts.

- Determine the personnel and equipment time-reporting requirements for each agency and/or organization involved in the response effort

- Ensure that all responders know of the time and method for submitting the daily time sheets

- Maintain a separate log to track overtime expenditures

- Work with the Cost Unit to agree on when the Cost Unit would like to receive the daily totals of personnel and equipment time reports and in what format

- Provide accurate time accounting to any Agency Representatives

- Track personnel and equipment hours against anticipated "burn-rate;" update "burn-rate" if necessary

- Determine need, and if approved, establish a commissary for the incident

- Provide completed time records to agencies that are demobilizing from the incident

- Maintain a Unit Log, ICS-214

Directions to the Procurement Unit Leader (PROC)

Timely contracting for services and supplies is critical to the response effort.

- Negotiate all contracts
- Establish local sources for equipment, supplies, and services and notify LSC
- Manage and account for all procurement orders
- Manage and account for all payments
- Document all contracts, procurement orders, and payments
- Report on the status of all contracts
- Administer all financial matters pertaining to vendor contracts
- Maintain a Unit Log, ICS-214

Directions to the Compensation/Claims Unit Leader (COMP)

One measure of how successfully a response is being managed is the attention that is paid to claims involving property that individuals make regarding damage from the response activities.

The Compensation/Claims Unit needs to act quickly on these claims so that there is no perception that the command team is not taking action. Documentation of responder injuries must also be timely and done with a high standard of care.

- Investigate all claims involving property associated with or involving the incident
- Investigate all incident accidents (e.g., vehicle accidents)
- Ensure that Unit personnel working on injury compensations are coordinating closely with the Medical Unit and the Safety Officer
- Develop and advertise incident claim process
- Maintain all files on injuries and illnesses associated with the incident
- Maintain thorough documentation on all claims (witness statements, photos, etc.)
- Report on the status of claims processing
- Maintain a Unit Log, ICS-214

Directions to the Cost Unit Leader (COST):

Incident Commanders/Unified Command are given wide latitude in determining how best to bring an incident under control.

The strategies and tactics that they employ early on may not be as scrutinized, but once a response shifts to more of a project phase the strategies that are used will have to be fiscally defensible. The Cost Unit can be a big help as they collect and analyze where the money is going.

- Ensure that personnel and equipment that will receive payment are properly identified
- Work with the Time and Procurement Units to get all cost data
- Conduct an analysis of costs and prepare estimates of incident costs
- Report on documented response costs and projected response costs
- Maintain accurate information on the actual cost of all assigned resources
- Identify and distribute the appropriate cost documentation forms
- Add up obligations from all sources (contractor, government, etc.) against each fund ceiling (for this reason, it will be important to understand fully the IC/UC decisions about which actions/contracts are directed to be made against which funding source)
- Monitor direct costs and anticipated costs and track the obligations against various ceilings on a daily basis
- Maintain a Unit Log, ICS-214

FSC Role in the ICS Planning Process

There are several meetings and briefings that you'll attend during each operational period as part of the ICS Planning Process. Be prepared for those meetings/briefings by referring to the various checklists below.

Command and General Staff Meeting

The Command and General Staff meeting will provide you with a lot of information on what is going on with regard to the direction of the response effort.

The Incident Commander/Unified Command will discuss their priorities, constraints and limitations, and incident objectives, and other items they want to communicate with you and the other members of the Command and General Staff.

You'll have the opportunity in this meeting to get clarification on any issues and provide a report on your Section's activities. Some items that you may want to bring up in this meeting include:

- Total incident costs
- Update on any claims
- Any injuries that require follow-on medical treatment
- Cost per day (burn-rate)
- Any contracting difficulties
- Any issues with receiving personnel and equipment hours

Planning Meeting

During the Planning Meeting, the Operations Section Chief (OSC) will brief the Incident Commander/Unified Command on his/her proposed tactical plan for the next operational period. What needs to come out of this meeting is that the IC/UC agrees to the OSC's plan and that you, as the FSC, as well as the other members of the Command and General Staff agree that you can support the plan. While in this meeting there are some things you want to do:

- Obtain information on resource requirements for cost considerations
- Identify high-cost operational resources
- Identify actions that may lead to potential claims
- Provide information on anticipated and known fiscal constraints

Operations Briefing

The Operations Briefing is conducted to brief oncoming operations personnel on their assignment for the operational period. This is your best opportunity to pass along to the field personnel any cost or claims issues that they need to be aware of as they go about their work. For example:

- Potential for liability claims
- What to do about problems with a contractor's performance
- How and when the FSC requires accounting of equipment and personnel hours
- Where you want any claims referred to (e.g., Compensation/Claims Unit)

TRANSFER OF COMMAND

Being prepared to conduct a Transfer of Command is an important responsibility of an Incident Commander (IC). Changing the leadership at the top during an emergency response has to be done as seamlessly as possible with minimum disruption to the response effort.

The need for Transfer of Command can occur when:

- A more qualified agency person arrives at the incident and assumes the role of Incident Commander

- The incident is under control and the Incident Commander role is being transferred back down to a less qualified individual

- The incident duration is such that an agency rotates their Incident Commanders on a rotation schedule that ensure sustainability

When command is transferred, the process must include a briefing that captures all essential information for continuing safe and effective operations. The Transfer of Command Briefing is critical to providing the incoming Incident Commander with an accurate assessment of on-scene operations. All personnel involved in the incident must be informed when a transfer of command has occurred.

Responsibilities of the Off-Going Incident Commander

When preparing for a Transfer of Command Briefing address the following:

- Negotiate a time and location for the Transfer of Command Briefing with the oncoming IC

- Designate someone to manage the on-scene operations while you're briefing the oncoming IC

- Determine who should attend the briefing in addition to the oncoming IC

- Ensure that the ICS-201/IAP is current and up-to-date with latest incident information

- If possible, provide a large map or chart of the incident area

- Organize your thoughts so that you know what you want to say

Checklist to guide the Transfer of Command Briefing

☐ If possible, make a copy of the ICS-201/IAP for your relief

☐ Use maps, charts, and other aids to point out locations and details about the incident

☐ Cover the current situation (provide incident overview as you see it)

☐ Cover initial response objectives and priorities

☐ Discuss current actions and tactics

☐ Review any planned actions that you were going to put into motion

☐ Review the current organization that you've established

☐ Discuss organizational changes you were considering

☐ Review how you're using the resources on-scene

☐ Provide a rundown of the resources that have been ordered and how they were going to support your planned actions

☐ Give a status of communications

☐ Summarize the briefing with your overall assessment of the incident's potential

Responsibilities of the On-Coming Incident Commander

The following is a Transfer of Command Briefing checklist for the on-coming Incident Commander:

- ☐ *Attempt to get out on the incident to get a firsthand assessment. Preferably do so with the off-going IC*

- ☐ *Agree on a time and place to conduct the Transfer of Command*

- ☐ *Get a copy of the ICS-201/IAP*

- ☐ *At a minimum try to get the following information:*
    - ☐ *Overall incident situation*
    - ☐ *Priorities and objectives*
    - ☐ *Agencies and jurisdictions involved*
    - ☐ *Incident organization*
    - ☐ *Facilities already established (including Staging Areas)*
    - ☐ *Information on committed resources*
    - ☐ *Resources ordered*
    - ☐ *Incident investigation*
    - ☐ *Communications schedule with supervisors*
    - ☐ *Political, media, environmental, and economic interest*
    - ☐ *Potential of the incident*
    - ☐ *List of any assisting and/or cooperating agencies*

- ☐ *Notify incident personnel once you have assumed the role of IC*

- ☐ *Ensure that the date and time of the transfer of command is recorded*

- ☐ *Consider reassigning the off-going IC to a new position on the incident (try not to lose his/her knowledge of the incident)*

- ☐ *Keep the ICS-201/IAP up-to-date as you make changes*

AREA COMMAND

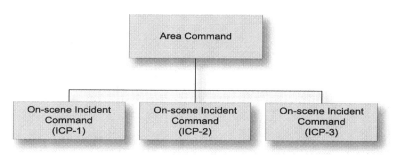

"Area Command in relationship to on-scene Incident Command"

The purpose of the Area Command (AC) is to provide oversight to multiple incident management teams, focusing primarily on strategic assistance and direction, and resolving competition for critical response resources. Area Command is an expansion of the Incident Command System and is specifically designed and developed to manage multiple on-scene incident management teams.

> "A critical resource is when there is more demand for certain kinds of resources (e.g., specialized teams, personnel, or equipment), than there is available supply. The limited or unavailability of a critical resource will have a direct negative impact on the overall management of the incident."

Note — Area Command does not replace the on-scene Incident Command's authority or responsibility. Execution of tactical operations remains the responsibility of the Incident Commander/Unified Command.

· All Hazard Field Guide ·

Determination to Activate an Area Command

An Agency Executive/Administrator can determine when an incident is of such magnitude, complexity, or operational intensity that it would benefit from the activation of an Area Command. Factors to consider when deciding to activate an Area Command include, but are not limited to:

- Complex incidents overwhelming local and regional government assets
- Overlapping jurisdictional boundaries
- An incident that crosses international borders
- The existence of, or the potential for, high-level national political and media interest
- Significant threat or impact to the public health and welfare, natural environment, property, or economy over a broad geographic area
- Difficulty with inter-incident resource allocation and coordination
- Major response activities occurring in multiple disciplines or with multiple incident management teams such as search and rescue, fire fighting, and environmental response

Area Command Organization

Area Command should never be involved in tactical operations; therefore an Operations Section is not required.

"Area Command is established by the Agency Executive/ Administrator who has authority over the Area Command"

Area Commander

The Area Commander has responsibility for overall strategic management of the incidents and will:

a. Establish Area Command strategic objectives

b. Establish overall response priorities

c. Communicate strategic direction to the Incident Commanders and make timely decisions

d. Allocate and track critical resources based on overall response priorities

e. Ensure that the incidents are properly managed

f. Ensure that the on-scene incident objectives are met

g. Help to resolve conflict with supporting agencies priorities

h. Communicate, at the commensurate level, with affected parties, stakeholders, and the public

i. Ensure that Agency Executive/Administrator direction is implemented

j. Ensure that appropriate incident information reporting requirements are met

k. Coordinate acquisition of off-incident, unassigned resources such as federal, state, local, and international resources, as appropriate

l. Develop and disseminate strategic guidance and planning information

m. Provide direction, guidance, and assistance to the support elements of the incident management teams

Area Command Liaison Officer

Establish liaison, as needed, with representatives of assisting and cooperating agencies. This will often be with the same agencies represented at the IC level, but will typically be a link to a more senior organizational level than that represented on-scene.

The major responsibilities of the Area Command Liaison Officer are:

a. Review Common Responsibilities in Chapter 2

b. Establish liaison, as needed, with stakeholders, such as environmental, economic, and political groups. It is expected, however, that the majority of stakeholder service and support will be handled by the on-scene command team

c. Support on-scene Liaison Officer efforts to establish strong ties with assisting/cooperating agencies and stakeholders

d. Maintain communications with stakeholders and assisting and cooperating agencies and keep Area Command advised of their issues and concerns

e. Liaise with all investigating agencies to minimize impact on incident response operations

f. With the AC PIO coordinate VIP site visits in an effort to minimize the impact to the on-scene IMTs

Area Command Public Information Officer

The Area Command Public Information Officer is responsible for developing and releasing information about the incident(s) to the news media, to incident personnel, and to other appropriate agencies and organizations.

Normally, detailed information regarding response specifics will be referred to and handled by the appropriate on-scene Public Information Officer (PIO). The Area Command Public Information Officer will generally provide information on overall progress and status of the response from a regional or national perspective.

The major responsibilities of the Area Command Public Information Officer are:

a. Review Common Responsibilities in Chapter 2

b. Provide information on the incident(s) to the media and other interested parties

c. Identify and communicate to AC organization and on-scene IMTs, the Area Command's policy and procedures for release of information

d. As directed, establish and manage the AC Joint Information Center

e. Coordinate with the on-scene PIO(s) to obtain information and to ensure consistency in release of information

f. Closely coordinate with on-scene PIO(s) to develop and establish an effective public information strategy

g. Evaluate public and media perception of the response effectiveness and keep AC and on-scene commands informed

h. Keep the AC and AC staff informed of news releases, press conferences, town meetings, etc., to be conducted at the AC level

i. Prepare briefing materials and coordinate the conduct of press conferences, town meetings, etc

j. Provide speaker preparation and coaching to members of the AC staff

k. With the AC Liaison Officer coordinate VIP site visits in an effort to minimize the impact on the on-scene IMTs

Area Command Safety Officer

The Area Command Safety Officer function is to develop and recommend measures for assuring personnel safety and to assess and/or anticipate hazardous and unsafe situations.

Detailed information regarding response specifics will be referred to and handled by the appropriate on-scene Safety Officer (SOF). The Area Command Safety Officer will generally provide information on overall safety issues and progress/status of the response from a regional or national perspective.

The major responsibilities of the Area Command Safety Officer are:

a. Review Common Responsibilities in Chapter 2

b. Develop AC Facility Safety Plan and monitor for compliance

c. Evaluate thoroughness of the on-scene Site Safety Plan(s)

d. As requested, provide assistance to on-scene SOFs and on-scene IMTs in investigating accidents, injuries, fatalities, etc

e. Review Incident Action Plans (IAPs) for safety implications

f. Work closely with regulatory organizations (e.g., OSHA, EPA, public health)

Area Command Intelligence Officer

The responsibility of the AC Intelligence Officer is to provide intelligence information for the AC that can have a direct impact on the response.

Detailed information regarding incident intelligence specifics will be referred to, and handled by, the appropriate on-scene Intelligence Officer. The AC Intelligence Officer will generally provide information on overall intelligence issues and progress/status of the response from a regional or national perspective.

The major responsibilities of the AC Intelligence Officer are:

a. Review Common Responsibilities in Chapter 2.

b. Working with AC, determine the level and complexity of intelligence needed to support its efforts

c. Reach agreement with AC on where the intelligence position will be located within the AC organization

d. Determine intelligence gaps and requirements needed to support AC's decision-making process and the development of the Operating Guide

e. Analyze and share intelligence among the AC organization, involved partners and the on-scene IMT(s)

f. Manage and process classified and unclassified requests for intelligence

g. Ensure that intelligence is properly used and filed

h. Coordinate intelligence gathering activities with external partners and organizations (e.g., FBI, state, local law enforcement)

Area Command Planning Chief (ACPC)

The AC Planning Chief is responsible for collecting, evaluating, managing, and disseminating incident information at the AC level. The responsibility of the ACPC is to provide AC planning information for the Area Command that can have a direct impact on the response personnel and influence the disposition of resources involved in the response.

Detailed information regarding incident planning specifics will be referred to and handled by the appropriate on-scene Planning Section Chief. The ACPC will generally provide information on overall planning issues and progress/status of the response from a regional or national perspective.

The major responsibilities of the ACPC are:

    a. Review Common Responsibilities in Chapter 2

    b. Review on-scene Incident Action Plans with purpose of assessing potential conflicts with AC direction

    c. Oversee the preparation and dissemination of the AC Operating Guide (ACOG)

    d. Facilitate AC meetings and briefings

    e. Prepare and conduct special situation briefings for AC

    f. Ensure appropriate displays are developed, maintained and posted

    g. Ensure all off-site reporting requirements are met, (e.g., ICS-209)

    h. Ensure a documentation process is in place for collecting, duplicating and filing information

i. Brief ACOG to AC staff, Agency Executives, On-scene Commanders, EOC, and JFO

j. Ensure that the On-scene Commanders are adequately anticipating and developing contingencies for addressing future response needs

k. Assist Area Commander/Unified Area Command in the development of strategies, objectives, priorities, operating procedures and protocols

l. Coordinate with AC Logistics on the identification of, ordering, assignment and demobilization of critical resources

m. Ensure accurate status and accounting of critical resources

n. Prepare and distribute the AC policies, procedures and decisions to the AC staff and on-scene ICs/UCs

o. Ensure a check-in process is in place to ensure accountability of visitors and command post personnel

p. Develop recommendations for demobilizing the AC organization

Area Command Situation Unit Leader

The Area Command Situation Unit Leader is responsible for collecting, processing and organizing incident information relating to the growth, mitigation or intelligence activities taking place on the incident. The responsibility of the Area Command Situation Unit Leader is to provide situational information to the AC.

The major responsibilities of the Area Command Situation Unit Leader are:

a. Review Common Responsibilities in Chapter 2

b. Develop and implement procedures for collecting and displaying the current operational picture that reflects AC overall response emphasis

c. Collect and analyze information gathered from On-scene Command, external entities, and AC staff, and brief AC on the potential implications

d. Maintain current situation status displays

e. Prepare incident situation information for support of, and use in, meetings, briefings and reporting documents

f. Prepare and conduct situation briefings

g. Establish and maintain an open action tracking process

h. Develop and maintain Incident Status Summary

i. As scheduled, provide frequent/timely incident status updates to Agency Executives, Emergency Operations Centers, Joint Field Office, and other entities as directed

j. Be prepared to respond to real-time critical information requests

k. As required, provide incident status updates to stakeholders or other external organizations on an unscheduled basis

l. Develop and post a briefing and meeting schedule

m. Develop a list of critical information elements

Area Command Critical Resources Unit Leader

The Area Command Critical Resources Unit Leader is responsible for maintaining the status of all critical tactical resources and personnel.

The Area Command Critical Resources Unit Leader will generally provide information on critical resources issues and progress/status of the response from a regional or national perspective.

> "A critical resource is when there is more demand for certain kinds of resources (e.g., specialized teams, personnel, or equipment), than there is available supply. The limited or unavailability of a critical resource will have a direct negative impact on the overall management of the incident."

The major responsibilities of the Area Command Critical Resources Unit Leader are:

a. Review Common Responsibilities in Chapter 2

b. Maintain resource status for all critical resources

c. Maintain resource status on all members of the AC organization

d. Establish and maintain a check-in process to ensure accountability of visitors and Area Command personnel

e. Develop and post an AC organization chart

f. Assist AC Planning Chief in the development of the ACOG

g. Support/assist the AC Planning Chief in assigning and demobilizing critical resources

h. Working with the On-scene Commands, submit critical resource needs to the AC Logistics Chief

i. Provide input to the AC Finance/Administration Chief to help track response costs for AC

j. Develop and maintain the Resource Allocation and Prioritization Worksheet ICS AC-215

k. Set-up meeting and briefing area using the meeting room layout

Area Command Documentation Unit Leader

The Area Command Documentation Unit Leader is responsible for the maintenance of accurate, up-to-date incident files.

The major responsibilities of the Area Command Documentation Unit Leader are:

a. Review Common Responsibilities in Chapter 2

b. Establish a process for collecting, analyzing and storing Area Command documentation

c. Establish duplication /copying service for AC organization

d. File all official memos, forms and reports

e. Enforce confidentiality policies on release of documents

f. Monitor accuracy and completeness of records submitted for filing

g. Provide duplicates of forms and reports to authorized requesters

h. Obtain approval for release of any documents or reports

i.   Prepare final files for hand-off to appropriate official for future use

j.   Document meetings

Area Command Logistics Chief

The responsibility of the Area Command Logistics Chief is to provide facilities, services, and materials to support Area Command operations.

The major responsibilities of the Area Command Logistics Chief are:

a.   Review Common Responsibilities in Chapter 2

b.   Establish and maintain an appropriate Area Command Post (ACP) for the AC organization

c.   Provide services and support for the AC organization, including billeting, transportation, feeding, etc

d.   Respond to requests to meet AC organization staffing requirements

e.   Establish and maintain a resource requesting and ordering process for the AC organization

f.   Work with on-scene Incident Management Teams to identify and respond to critical resource needs

g.   Identify list of potential critical/specialized resource suppliers

h.   Source, order and track critical and specialized resources from point of departure to incident check-in

i.   Support/assist the ACPC, in developing recommendations for establishing priorities to govern the assignment and demobilization of critical resources

j. Plan for, and establish secure and non-secure voice and data communication for internal and external needs of the AC organization

k. As appropriate, provide security services for the ACP

l. When directed by AC, take charge of the expanded supply network to support the on-scene commanders

m. Develop AC Communications Plan, ICS AC-205

n. Establish and maintain an accountable-property tracking system

o. Initiate and maintain a AC phone directory

p. Coordinate directly with the AC Finance/Administration Chief, for procurement and accounting purposes

Area Command Facilities Unit Leader

The Area Command Facilities Unit Leader is primarily responsible for the set up, maintenance and demobilization of AC facilities.

The major responsibilities of the Area Command Facilities Unit Leader are:

a. Review Common Responsibilities in Chapter 2

b. Determine space requirements for Area Command Post (ACP)

c. Prepare ACP footprint and assist AC staff in setting up individual work areas

d. Coordinate with AC Safety Officer in conducting site safety inspection of ACP

e. If required, provide for billeting, feeding, and transportation of AC personnel

f. Provide for facility maintenance (e.g., sanitation, janitorial services, lighting)

g. Ensure facility is maintained in a safe condition

h. Once AC stands down and deactivates, restore facility to its pre-occupancy condition

i. If required, develop Facility Security Plan and manage security activities including staff parking area

j. Ensure that all facility equipment is acquired, setup and properly functioning (e.g., furniture, display boards, copy machines, faxes)

k. Establish property accountability system for issued equipment

Area Command Communications Unit Leader

The AC Communications Unit Leader is responsible for developing plans for the effective use of AC communications equipment and facilities; installing and testing of communications equipment; and supervision of the AC Communications Center.

The major responsibilities of the Area Command Communications Unit Leader are:

   a. Review Common Responsibilities in Chapter 2

   b. Prepare and implement AC Communications Plan (ICS-205a) for both internal and external needs

   c. Provide input into the ACOG as it relates to communications

   d. Ensure communications systems are installed, tested and maintained

   e. Coordinate with on-scene Communications Unit Leaders and assist with acquisition of specialized equipment and communication frequency management issues

   f. Provide technical information and support to both the AC staff and IMTs

   g. Establish accountability system for issued communications equipment

   h. If required, install secure communications networks

Area Command Information Technology Specialists

The major responsibilities of the Area Command Information Technology Specialists are:

a. Review Common Responsibilities in Chapter 2

b. Analyze the requirements for data processing to support the Area Command Post (ACP) for both internal and external data transmission needs (for both secure and non-secure transmissions)

c. Install and maintain ACP Local Area Nework (LAN) and standalone system including laptops, printers and plotters

d. Brief user groups on system and network operations

e. Based on requirements, determine need for specialized expertise to operate and maintain systems

f. Implement property accountability

Area Command Finance/Administration Chief

The AC Finance/Administration Chief is responsible for all financial, administrative and cost analysis aspects of the AC and for supervising members of the AC Finance/Administration Section.

The major responsibilities of the AC Finance/Administration Chief are:

a. Review Common Responsibilities in Chapter 2

b. Determine Area Command requirements for cost accounting

c. Coordinate with on-scene Finance/Administration Section Chief(s) to determine methodology for reporting cost information

d. Collect, analyze and summarize cost data

e. Keep AC briefed on response costs

f. Ensure that response costs are managed within the established financial ceilings and guidelines

g. Coordinate and advise AC on ceiling adjustments when necessary

h. Coordinate with Joint Field Office for Stafford Act funding sources

i. If required, develop cost sharing agreements with participating members of the AC

j. Monitor use of high-cost specialized equipment and keep AC advised

k. If required, coordinate processing of claims, resulting from response actions

l. Oversee contract management

Optional Positions/Technical Specialists

Two AC positions that the Area Commander/Unified Area Command may add to their team are a Legal and a Security Officer. Ready access to the expertise and advice of a legal and security professional will dictate whether to add those functions to the Command Staff.

Legal Specialist

a. Review Common Responsibilities in Chapter 2

b. Advise the AC on legal issues

c. Review documents developed by AC or AC staff to ensure they meet the legal requirements of participating agencies and organizations

d. Ensure documentation control system in place

e. Identify what documents and/or information can or cannot be released during the response

Security Specialist

a. Review Common Responsibilities in Chapter 2

b. Determine security requirements for the ACP

c. Develop and implement ACP Security Plan

d. Obtain assets to monitor and enforce security

e. If required, determine need for ACP identification badge system and provide this service

f. Evaluate and recommend to AC the need for secure communications for both voice and data

g. Coordinate with on-scene security specialist(s) as needed to ensure security requirements are met

h. If needed, establish a list of ACP personnel along with their levels of security clearance

Aviation Coordinator

   a. Review Common Responsibilities in Chapter 2

   b. Discuss with AC where in the organization this function will be assigned

   c. Determine AC requirements for use of aviation assets

   d. If aviation assets are determined to be a critical resource, coordinate with the Planning and Logistics Chief on ordering, assigning and demobilizing these assets

   e. Schedule the use of aviation assets assigned to support AC and their staff

   f. Coordinate with the on-scene Air Operations Branch Directors for multi- incident use of air assets

   g. Provide technical expertise on the use of specialized air assets for both AC and on-scene IMT(s)

   h. If needed, develop an ICS-220, Air Operations Summary Work Sheet

Documentation Specialist/Executive Assistant

a. Review Common Responsibilities in Chapter 2

b. Determine AC requirements for documenting meetings and briefings

c. Prepare decision memos for AC and primary staff review and approval

d. Ensure AC meeting notes are inclusive

e. Ensure that AC meeting notes, memos and reports are provided to the Documentation Unit Leader

f. Develop and maintain chronological log of AC decisions, direction and actions

g. Perform other administrative duties as assigned

h. Coordinate with legal specialist on document preparation requirements and documentation preservation protocols

Area Command Operating Cycle

As with the incident management teams that are conducting tactical operations, the AC team follows a prescribed process for developing and implementing strategic direction to ensure that the incident management teams under its direction are well-supported and coordinated. The process is called the Area Command Operating Cycle.

Area Command Operating Cycle

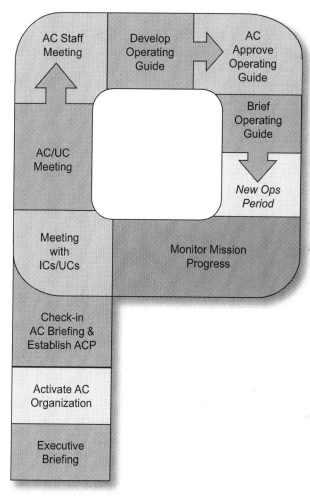

"AC Operating Cycle"

Executive Briefing

This is the first activity in the AC Operating Cycle where the representatives in Area Command are briefed by senior agency executives on the overall situation.

Use the following agenda to help guide your briefing.

Facilitator: Senior Agency Executive or designee

Attendees: Selected Area Commanders and deputies

Executive Briefing Agenda

1. Brief on the need and requirements for an AC organization

2. Discuss prior communications between executives and ICs/UCs

3. Brief on current situation

4. Brief on AC authorities, duties, and responsibilities

5. Discuss overarching political, social, economic, and environmental issues affecting the mission or the response

6. Clarify reporting and briefing requirements (including critical information) and lines of authority

7. Discuss and reach agreement on overall AC staffing and Area Command Post (ACP) location

8. Discuss plans and agreements that may or will be in place

9. Close out meeting with concurrence from Area Commanders that their concerns have been addressed

"Executive Briefing Agenda"

As the Area Commander, during the Executive Briefing, you want a thorough briefing. Use the list below as a memory jogger for some of the important items you want addressed.

- *Scope of your authority*
- *Reporting relationships and responsibilities*
- *Your organization's/agency's priorities*
- *Cost constraints*
- *Critical information reporting thresholds (e.g., serious accidents and/or injuries, loss of life, major operational accomplishments or impediments)*
- *When the AC is expected to be operational*
- *Briefing schedule and content for Agency Executive updates*
- *Any political, social, economic, and/or environmental concerns*
- *If pre-determined, location of the Area Command Post*
- *If you will be working in a Unified Area Command, who are the other agencies with Area Commanders with whom you will be working*
- *Other support facilities that are being activated (e.g., Emergency Operations Center (EOC), Joint Field Office (JFO))*
- *Names of assigned Incident Commanders and locations of Incident Command Posts that you will be managing*
- *What is the AC's geographic area of responsibility*

Activate AC Organization

Once you have received your Agency Executive briefing, you will need to take some time to determine the initial level of staffing that will be required to establish an effective Area Command organization.

If you are working in a Unified Area Command (where there is more than one Area Commander), decisions on staffing and what agencies will fill which Area Command positions will have to be agreed upon.

In addition to staffing, you will have to determine where to establish your Area Command Post (ACP) unless your Agency Executive has already decided that in advance.

Use the following agenda to help guide the activation of the AC organization.

Facilitator: AC Member or ACPC (if available)

Attendees: Area Commanders

Activate AC Organization Agenda

1. Facilitator brings meeting to order, covers ground rules and reviews agenda

2. Validate makeup of newly formed Unified Area Command (UAC)

3. Clarify UAC roles and responsibilities

4. Review agency policies and AC authorities

5. Establish and document response priorities, limitations and constraints

6. Define and document the UAC jurisdictional boundaries and focus (Area(s) of Responsibility)

7. Determine location of Area Command Post (see following page)

8. Determine the AC operational period length/start time and work shift hours

9. Designate lead organization for AC Planning Chief, Information, Safety, Intelligence and Liaison Officers as needed

10. Designate other AC key staff assignments as needed

11. Discuss and agree on managing sensitive information, resource ordering, cost sharing, cost accounting, and operational security issues

12. Summarize and document key decisions, procedures and guidance

"Activate AC Organization Agenda"

Guidance for selecting an Area Command Post

There are some guidelines that you should try to follow when selecting the location of the ACP. To help you make the best choice for locating the ACP, consider the following in your decision making:

- The ACP should be strategically positioned in close proximity to the incidents that you are overseeing

- You do not want to co-locate your ACP with one of the Incident Management Teams. The reasons for this are:
  - It is difficult to maintain a clear delineation between the Area Command and Incident Commander's responsibilities
  - There may be a perception of favoritism since you are co-located with one incident management team and not the others
  - It may become difficult to separate the day-to-day activities that are occurring within both the Area Command and the Incident Command; this invites confusion

- The location that you select for the Area Command Post should have:
  - Sufficient space for your team with the ability to expand should it become necessary
  - Adequate communications capability to enable you to communicate with the Incident Command/Unified Commands, Emergency Operations Centers, Agency Executives, Joint Information Center, and Joint Field Office
  - Adequate backup power to enable 24 x 7 operations
  - Adequate secure parking
  - Safe and secure work environment
  - Close proximity to a Heliport

Check-in, Area Command Briefing, and Establish the Area Command Post

At this "step" in the Area Command Operating Cycle, your initial Area Command team members begin to check-in and it is important for you to give them a good situational briefing. Make sure that the briefing includes:

- The current situation
- Area Command's roles and responsibilities in supporting incident operations
- Your expectations
- Initial direction and guidance that you want your team to follow
- Clarification on the overall scope of the assignment
- Reporting relationships with the Incident Command/ Unified Commands, Emergency Operations Centers (EOC), and Joint Field Office (JFO)

Ensure that you establish some interim operating procedures such as:

- Critical resource ordering and tracking
- Critical information reporting
- Hours of operation and command post staffing
- Meeting and briefing schedule

Once the Area Command team reports that they are prepared to support incident operations you want to notify the Agency Executive, Incident Commanders/ Unified Command, EOC, and JFO that your Area Command is operational.

Use the following agenda to help guide the initial briefing to the AC staff.

Facilitator: ACPC or Area Commander(s) with participation from Planning and Logistics Chiefs

Attendees: All AC personnel

AC Briefing Agenda

1. AC Planning Chief brings meeting to order, conducts roll call, covers ground rules and reviews agenda

2. AC SITL conducts situation status briefing

3. AC provides initial comments, expectations, initial assignments, and closing comments

---

"AC Briefing Agenda"

Meeting with the IC/UC

With your Area Command Post established and your team prepared to support the incidents, you are ready for perhaps one of the most important "steps" in the Area Command Operating Cycle – meeting the Incident Commanders.

If at all possible, try to have your first meeting with the Incident Commanders face-to-face (follow-on meetings can be by telephone or video conference) and with all of the Incident Commanders present.

The first meeting is a golden opportunity to establish a positive working relationship between your Area Command team and the on-scene commands.

You want to walk out of this meeting with a good situational picture of each of the incidents along with a list of critical resources. These two items (incident situation and critical resources) will enable you to start making some hard decisions as to which of the on-scene incident management teams will have priority for receiving the resources that have been identified as critical.

Use the following agenda to help guide your meeting.

Facilitator: ACPC

Attendees: Area Commanders, AC Planning, Logistics and Finance/Admin Chiefs, On-scene ICs/UCs and their Planning Section Chiefs

Meeting with the IC/UC Agenda

1. ACPC brings meeting to order, conducts roll call, and reviews agenda

2. ACs provide opening remarks along with policy direction, Agency Executives' expectations, AC interim operating procedures, and ground rules

3. ACPC provides guidance on information reporting, including timeframes, units of measure and formats along with critical information reporting

4. AC Logistics Chief provides guidance on ordering and sharing of specialized and critical resources, including demobilization of these resources

5. AC Finance/Administration Chief provides guidance on cost accounting, reporting injuries and accidents

6. ICs/UCs report on their individual situation to include resources at risk, incident objectives, incident priorities, constraints, limitations, resources required and consequences if resource requirements are not met

7. Resolve oustanding issues or concerns

8. ACPC solicits final comments and adjourns the meeting

"Meeting with the IC/UC Agenda"

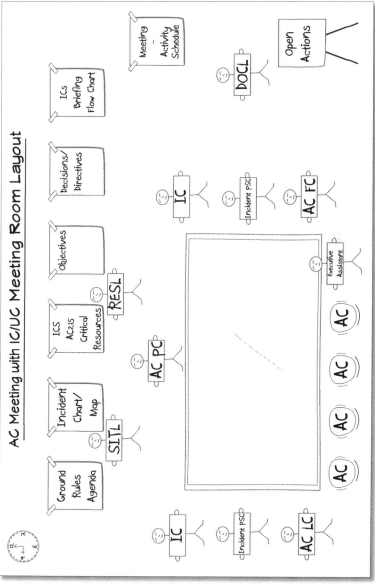

"AC meeting with IC/UC Meeting Room Layout"

As an Area Commander, one of the most important responsibilities that you have is deciding how best to allocate the critical resources. When you meet with the ICs consider having your AC Planning Chief (ACPC) begin filling in the AC Resource Allocation and Prioritization Worksheet, ICS AC-215. The ACPC should be documenting on the ICS AC-215 those resources that the ICs have identified as essential to their mission and being in short supply and high demand – critical resources.

Using the ICS AC-215, Area Command Resource Allocation and Prioritization Worksheet

The ICS AC-215 is designed to enable the AC staff to record critical resource requirements and to determine the number of critical resources that are needed to meet the requirements of the on-scene IMTs.

Following, is an example of upper left corner of the ICS AC-215 that has been filled in with the process for completing the various blocks.

Block 1 — Area Command Identifier: This is where you record the name of the AC (e.g., St. Louis Area Command)

Block 4 — Incident Priority: In the event that Area Command designates the various incidents under its command based on priority, Block 4 is where you would note which of the incidents was priority one, two, three, etc.

The majority of the time, the Area Command sets priorities for which incident is first in line to receive a particular critical resource and does not designate an entire incident as having priority over another.

Block 5 — Incidents: In this block you list the names of the various incidents that fall under the responsibility of your Area Command (e.g., Arch)

AREA COMMAND RESOURCE ALLOCATION AND PRIORITIZATION WORKSHEET

6. CRITICAL KINDS OF RESOURCES

1. AREA COMMAND IDENTIFIER: St. Louis Area Command	4. INCIDENT PRIORITY / 5. INCIDENTS		US&R task force	Ambulance Type I
	Arch	REQ	3	10
		HAVE	1	5
		NEED	2	5
		RESOURCE PRIORITY	2	1
	University City	REQ	2	7
		HAVE	0	4
		NEED	2	3
		RESOURCE PRIORITY	1	3

"Upper left corner of a filled-in ICS AC -215"

Block 6 — Kinds of Critical Resources: This is where you record the kind of resources that are determined to be critical. For example, one kind of resource that might be identified as critical are the FEMA Urban Search and Rescue (US&R) task forces.

Once the critical resources are identified, the Incident Commanders will tell you how many of those critical resources that he or she will require to accomplish his or her objectives. Your staff should record that information on the ICS AC-215.

- **REQ**: For each critical resource that is identified (in this example, FEMA US&R task forces) you want to ensure that you record the number of US&R task forces that each of the incidents require (REQ). For the Arch Incident, the number of US&R task forces required is three (3). One thing to remember is that although you have several incidents working under you, not all of them may require US&R task forces.

- **HAVE**: Once you know the number of US&R task forces that are required, you want to know how many US&R task forces are currently assigned to each of the incidents. For the Arch Incident, the number of US&R task forces that the incident has assigned to it is one (1).

- **NEED**: The NEED is simply the difference between the number of US&R task forces that the Arch Incident requires and the number of US&R task forces that the Arch Incident already has checked into the incident.

- **RESOURCE PRIORITY**: The resource priority block is used to record the Area Command's decision as to how it will prioritize the incidents that will have precedence in receiving a critical resource. In our example, the Arch Incident is priority two (2) for US&R task forces.

AREA COMMAND RESOURCE ALLOCATION AND PRIORITIZATION WORKSHEET

1. AREA COMMAND IDENTIFIER: **St. Louis Area Command**

6. KINDS OF CRITICAL RESOURCES

5. INCIDENTS	4. INCIDENT PRIORITY		US&R task force	Ambulance Type I
Arch		REQ	3	10
		HAVE	1	5
		NEED	2	5
		RESOURCE PRIORITY	2	1
University City		REQ	2	7
		HAVE	0	4
		NEED	2	3
		RESOURCE PRIORITY	1	3

"Upper left corner of a filled-in ICS AC -215"

Example of Using Criteria to Help Determine Resource Priorities

As an Area Commander, it is important to document the criteria that you used to help guide your decision as to why one incident is given a higher priority for a critical resource over another incident.

You may have received criteria from your Agency Administrator/Executive during your briefing or you may develop some of your own criteria like those listed below:

- Safety of Life
- Numbers of lives at risk
- Risk to responders versus benefit
- Time sensitivity (limited window of opportunity)
- Higher probability of success

Following is an example of upper right corner of the ICS AC-215 that has been filled in.

Block 7 — Comments: Record briefly some of the relevant information that the Area Command will use to determine where the greatest benefit will be gained when assigning critical resources.

		2. DATE & TIME PREPARED	3. OPERATING CYCLE (DATE & TIME)
		12 October 0900	12 Oct 1800 To 13 Oct 1800
US&R task force	Ambulance Type I		7. COMMENTS
3	10		Hundreds of injured are reported throughout the incident area.
1	5		Hazards in collapsed building structures will significantly
2	5		impede search-and-rescue operations and present a high degree of danger to rescue efforts.
2	1		
2	7		Several reinforced concrete high-rise apartment buildings are
0	4		heavily damaged with a high number of trapped victims. Initial assessment indicates a high degree of success if US&R task
2	3		forces are committed to the incident.
1	3		

"Upper right corner of a filled-in ICS AC -215"

22-41

What happens when an incident no longer requires a critical resource

When an incident no longer requires a critical resource such as an Urban Search and Rescue Task Force, Area Command is to be notified. This will enable Area Command to re-direct the critical resource to another incident management team that has been waiting for it to be available.

If there is no longer a need for the critical resource, the incident that has the excess critical resource will demobilize it under the Area Command's direction. Area Command needs to ensure that the Incident Commanders are briefed on how excess critical resources will be demobilized.

AC Unified Command Meeting

The Unified Area Command will use the information derived from the IC meeting to develop overall strategies, objectives, priorities and identify any critical resource needs or issues the AC will have to manage.

Unified Area Command

The agencies that make up a Unified Area Command may closely mirror the agencies that make up the Unified Command on-scene. For example, if the Unified Command on scene is made up of the fire department, law enforcement, public works, and emergency medical services, the Unified Area Command may have a similar makeup.

This is important because when Area Command is making critical resource allocation decisions that are directly impacting on-scene operations you want senior officials from those agencies to be involved in the decision making.

Best practices for a successful Unified Area Command

- Each Area Commander must have the authority to speak for his or her agency and to commit resources and funds

- Area Commanders must collectively agree on an overall direction, priorities, objectives, and decisions

- Each Area Commander's jurisdictional authority is not compromised or neglected

- Each Area Commander should stay focused on providing strategic direction and avoid getting down "into the weeds" on issues

Use the following agenda to help guide your meeting.

Facilitator: AC Planning Chief

Attendees: Area Commanders and other staff upon AC request

AC Unified Command Meeting Agenda

1. ACPC brings meeting to order

2. AC addresses any policies, limitations and constraints

3. AC reaches agreement on criteria for identifying critical resources

4. AC discusses and prioritizes incidents

5. ACPC facilitates discussion to develop overall response priorities

6. ACPC leads discussion on development of strategic objectives

7. AC will also finalize the AC operating procedures, (e.g., core hours of operation, night watch, staffing requirements, meeting schedules, reporting timeframes)

8. AC identifies any specific tasks for AC staff

9. AC addresses any critical issues derived from the IC/UC Meeting or Agency Executive Briefing

"AC Unified Command Meeting Agenda"

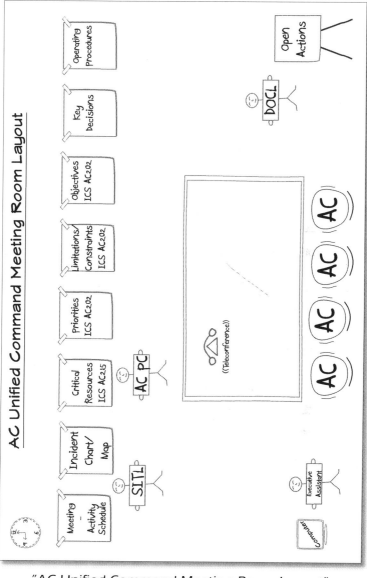

"AC Unified Command Meeting Room Layout"

Area Command Staff Meeting

The effort you put into providing clear direction and expectations to your staff at the outset of the response will payoff and reduce confusion and frustration.

Use the following agenda to help guide your meeting.

Facilitator: AC Planning Chief

Attendees: Area Commanders and AC staff to include Unit Leaders and Technical Specialists, if needed

Area Command Staff Meeting Agenda

1. ACPC brings meeting to order, conducts roll call, covers ground rules, and reviews agenda

2. AC SITL conducts situation status briefing

3. AC provides comments

4. AC presents:

   a. Any decisions that have been made (e.g., prioritizing the assignment of critical resources, ACP hours of operation)

   b. The assignment of any tasks that must be accomplished (e.g., immediately initiate the critical resource ordering process)

   c. The internal and external reporting process for the AC

   d. A media and stakeholder outreach strategy

   e. The AC meeting and activity schedule

   f. Overall impacts on AC organization (agreed upon shift in workload from Incidents to AC)

continued...

... cont'd

    g. Expectations for documentation

    h. Review of the AC Operating Guide

    i. Review of AC staffing to ensure it is robust enough to provide appropriate incident support

    j. Review of AC decisions and direction

    k. Discussion of potential issues (e.g., potential push back from some community leaders who disagree with resource allocation process)

    l. Identification of any limitations and constraints that Area Command is operating under (e.g., time constraints for obtaining enough life saving resources within the possible window of opportunity)

5. ACPC facilitates a short discussion on issues and concerns and adjourns meeting

"Area Command Staff Meeting Agenda"

Area Command Staff Meeting Room Layout

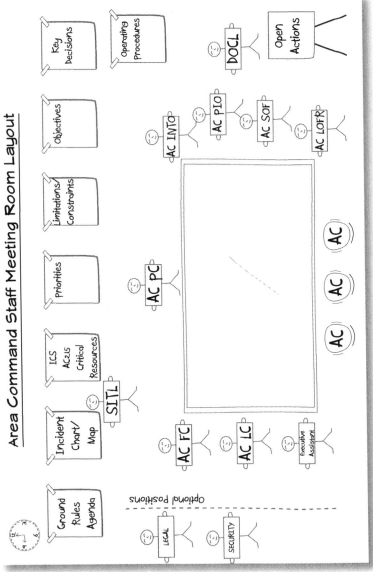

"Area Command Staff Meeting Room Layout"

Develop Operating Guide

During this block of time, the AC staff develops components that are to be included in the Operating Guide. These components must be developed in time to meet the deadlines set by the Planning Chief so Planning can assemble the Operating Guide. The deadline must be early enough to permit timely AC review, approval and duplication.

Area Command Operating Guide

The Area Command Operating Guide is a guidance document that should help to ensure that all players remain focused on what the Area Command roles and responsibilities are, and how they will be implemented.

The Area Command Operating Guide is similar to the Incident Action Plan that is produced by on-scene incident management teams.

The Operating Guide is designed to provide strategic direction and support to the Incident Commanders and to ensure that the Area Command organization's activities are coordinated with the incidents under its command.

The actual contents of an Operating Guide will vary depending on the situation, the Area Commander's preference, and external influences such as Emergency Operations Centers and a Joint Field Office.

Example of Area Command Operating Guide Contents

Saint Louis Area Command Operating Guide

Contents

- Area Command Priorities
- Area Command Objectives
- Area Command Management Philosophies
- Safety Message
- Key Decisions
- Response Emphasis
- Area Command Organization Chart
- Daily Activities Schedule
- Daily Conference Call Agenda
- Critical Resource Allocation
- AC Communications Plan
- Medical Plan
- Phone Directory

"Example of AC Operating Guide contents"

Area Command Approves Operating Guide

Once the Operating Guide has been put together, the AC Planning Chief will present it to command for approval.

Take time to review the Operating Guide to ensure that it represents the direction and expectations that command established. The Guide should provide information that helps to ensure close coordination between Area Command and incident management teams.

Remember that the Operating Guide is part of the incident documentation that will survive well into the future, so make sure that when you place your signature on it, that it meets your standards.

Brief Operating Guide Agenda

The AC Planning Chief will make sure that everyone has a copy of the Guide and will facilitate the briefing. Command's responsibility is to provide any motivational remarks and be prepared to provide clarification on the contents of the Guide.

Briefing to on-scene ICs/UCs may be accomplished by video conferencing or some other medium. Copies are either faxed or sent electronically to on-scene ICs/UCs and Agency Executives.

Use the following agenda to help guide your briefing.

Facilitator: AC Planning Chief

Attendees: All AC staff and if possible on-scene ICs/ UCs, and Agency Executives

Briefing the Operating Guide Agenda

1. AC Planning Chief opens meeting, conducts roll call and reviews agenda

2. AC SITL conducts situation status briefing and provides projections as needed

3. AC provides opening remarks

4. AC Planning Chief presents Operating Guide

5. AC Logistics Chief presents status of specialized and critical resources

6. AC Finance/Administration Chief presents status of cost tracking and other cost accounting issues

7. AC Planning Chief conducts (round robin) to clarify and resolve open issues with participants

8. AC Planning Chief adjourns briefing

"Brief Operating Guide Agenda"

Area Command Brief Operating Guide Room Layout

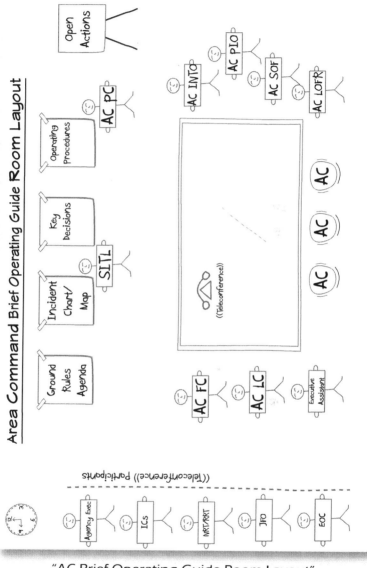

"AC Brief Operating Guide Room Layout"

Monitor Mission Progress

Assessment is a continuous process to help determine needed adjustments to the Operating Guide and assist in planning future support to the incident management teams.

Following the AC Operating Guide briefing and shift change, all AC staff will review mission progress and make recommendations to the AC. This feedback/ information is continuously gathered from various sources.

As the approved Operating Guide is implemented, the Area Command team will:

- Monitor and respond to progress and needs of the incident management teams
- Develop and use strategic planning tools such as projections, models, forecasts, and other similar information
- Review effectiveness of the Operating Guide and make appropriate changes
- Maintain liaison with entities supporting or coordinating with the AC
- Conduct meetings and briefings
- Ensure situation reports are timely
- Maintain document control system
- Ensure critical information reporting is being conducted
- Review AC organization staffing
- Maintain status of critical resources
- Maintain close coordination with their counterparts on the incident management teams
- Review and revise operating procedures as needed

Area Command Coordination

As an Area Commander, you may have to work with many entities in order to effectively support the Incident Commanders/Unified Command under your command.

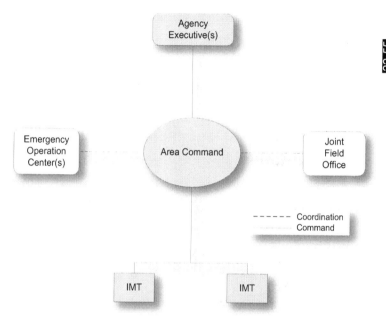

"Area Command coordinates with several entities such as Emergency Operations Centers and a Joint Field Office to support the on-scene incident management teams."

When working with Emergency Operations Centers (EOC) and a Joint Field Office (JFO), Area Command will provide:

- The current status of the situation on each incident under its command, providing a common operating picture for incidents under its jurisdiction

- Any critical resources that the incident(s) need but that can not be filled

The coordination relationship between Area Command and the EOC and JFO is a two-way street. EOCs and the JFO provide the needed resources and technical expertise to Area Command in support of the Incident Commanders.

BRANCH TACTICAL PLANNING

Usually, tactical planning will be conducted by the Operations Section Chief (OSC) at the Incident Command Post. However, there are circumstances when the complexity of an incident requires that specific tactical planning is conducted at the Branch level within the Operations Section.

The OSC and Planning Section Chief (PSC) will determine if Branch Tactical Planning is appropriate for the situation. Some examples of circumstances that may lead them to use this technique include:

- Security classification level of a particular tactical operation such as a vehicle accident where the transport of nuclear weapons is involved.

- During the initial phase of an incident, when the incident situation is not well known and the Planning Section is not robust.

- The technical qualifications necessary to do effective planning resides with the tactical asset (e.g., diving operations, SWAT, high angle rescue, US&R).

- Geographic separation from the Incident Command Post makes it impractical to have tactical planning done at the ICP.

The Branch Director, working closely with the Planning Section and Safety Officer goes through the same tactical planning process as the Operations Section Chief - completing an ICS-215 Operational Planning Worksheet. The OPBD works with the Safety Officer to analyze the hazards with the proposed plan of action, and in completing the ICS-204 Assignment List for each function that is the responsibility of the Branch.

For Branch Tactical Planning to be effective there must be a strong exchange of information and support between the Branch and the Incident Command Post (ICP). The Branch must continually communicate information on Branch activities, progress, constraints, effectiveness, and support needs.

The support needs in particular must be communicated as soon as they are identified at the Branch level in order for the appropriate staff elements within the ICP to address them. The staff within the ICP must be sensitive to the circumstances within the Branch and ensure that timely, accurate and effective support is provided.

When Branch Tactical Planning is used, the Planning Section provides key support.

- Interpretation of Command's Direction
- Strategy information
- Information from existing contingency plans
- Resource and situation status information
- Modeling and prediction information (including weather)
- Personnel and materials (e.g., maps, diagrams, forms) to support the planning effort
- Technical Specialist as needed

Branch Tactical Planning Development Checklist

Planning Section

- Resource tracking of Branch assets (e.g., Check-in, demobilization)
- Incident situation update requirements (e.g., FOBS, situation reporting to ICP)
- GIS mapping capabilities
- Modeling (ALOHA, CAMEO, NARAC)
- Meteorological forecast
- Technical Specialist
- Resource ordering of Branch assets (who will do it)
- Branch level incident documentation
- Reporting requirements between the Branch and Planning (e.g., how often, method)
- Support plan development (e.g., incident evacuation plans, decontamination plans)
- Contingency plans (e.g., an incident within an incident)
- Planning support material (e.g., forms, T-cards)

Logistics Section

- Incident communications management in support of the development of the Incident Action Plan form ICS-205, Incident Communications Plan (e.g., frequencies assignment, secure communications)
- Medical Plan (ICS-206)
- What facilities are required to support the Branch?
- What level of incident support facility security is required?

Operations Section Chief

- *Communicates Command's direction (e.g., decisions, priorities)*
- *Collection of operational effectiveness reports from the Branch*
- *Provides assistance and support in developing strategies*
- *Delineation of authority between OSC and Branch Director (OPBD)*
- *Air Operations support*
- *Reporting thresholds (e.g., critical information)*
- *Coordination with other Command and General Staff as needed to maximize effectiveness and efficiency of Branch operations*

Safety Officer

- *Assignment of Assistant Safety Officer(s)*

- *Site Safety Plan development and implementation*

- *Management of PPE issue, use, and disposal for the Branch*

- *Coordination with Medical Unit Leader and other medical entities as necessary to assure most expeditious access to medical services for Branch personnel*

- *Provide safety input into Branch planning process and IAP documents*

- *Agreement on the authority of Assistant Safety Officers from the Safety Officer*

- *Safety reporting requirements back to the ICP Branch Tactical Planning Process*

Branch Tactical Planning Process

The "steps" below outline the Branch Tactical Planning Process (see opposite Planning "P") that will help guide the planning effort at the Branch level.

1. OSC and PSC agree that Branch Tactical Planning is appropriate for the situation. OSC and PSC advise IC/UC and seek approval to conduct Branch Tactical Planning.

2. OSC and PSC in consultation with the affected Branch(es) determine the level of planning support required to effectively conduct Branch Tactical Planning. OPBD and Assistant Safety Officer develop an ICS-215 and ICS-215a for all Divisions, Groups, and Staging Areas under the Branch.

3. The OPBD develops specific ICS-204s for each work assignment identified on the ICS-215. The ICS-204s developed by the OPBD will be included in the Incident Action Plan (see note below). The PSC will ensure that the ICS-204s submitted by the OPBD include resources, work assignment, communications, logistical support and safety.

   In addition to the specific ICS-204s, the OPBD will develop a summary ICS-204 that covers the overall operations of the Branch for the OSC's approval.

4. The OSC will brief the branch's assignment from a strategic level and the OPBD will conduct the detailed field briefing to their DIVS and STAM.

5. The OSC, PSC, and OPBD assess and monitor the implementation of the Branch Tactical Planning effort and make necessary corrections.

NOTE: — If the tactical operations are classified, the OSC may choose to only include in the IAP the Branch Level ICS-204 that summarizes all of the Branch's operations. This can help protect classified information while still ensuring that all operations are in the Incident Action Plan.

Branch Tactical Planning Process

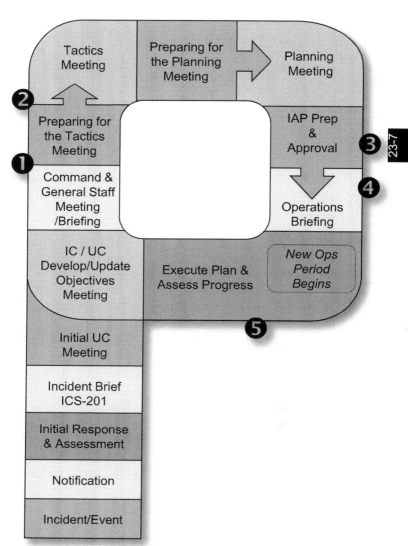

"Branch Tactical Planning Process"

Example of a Specific ICS-204

1. BRANCH	2. ~~DIVISION~~ / GROUP	**ASSIGNMENT LIST**
Fire/Rescue	Fire Suppression	

3. INCIDENT NAME	4. OPERATIONAL PERIOD (Date and Time)
Denver RDD	12 July 0600 to 12 July 1800

5. OPERATIONS PERSONNEL

OPERATIONS CHIEF _B. Roberts_ ~~DIVISION~~/GROUP SUPERVISOR _J. Nester_

BRANCH DIRECTOR _R. Russell_ AIR TACTICAL GROUP SUPERVISOR_____

6. RESOURCES ASSIGNED THIS PERIOD

STRIKE TEAM/TASK FORCE RESOURCE DESIGNATOR	EMT	LEADER	NUMBER PERSONS	TRANS NEEDED	DROP OFF POINT/TIME	PICK UP POINT/TIME
Fire Suppression TF-1	Y	M. Yale	21		Elitch Staging 0530	Elitch Staging 1830
Fire Suppression TF-2	Y	M. Strong	21		Elitch Staging 0530	Elitch Staging 1830
DFD Engine ST-7 (Type I)		L. Brown	21		Elitch Staging 0530	Elitch Staging 1830
DFD Engine ST-4 (Type I)		K. Andrews	21		Elitch Staging 0530	Elitch Staging 1830
Heavy Rescue Company 3		V. Holloway	4		Elitch Staging 0530	Elitch Staging 1830
Heavy Rescue Company 1		A. Bushu	4		Elitch Staging 0530	Elitch Staging 1830

7. WORK ASSIGNMENTS

Continue fire suppression operations throughout the incident area. Take initial steps in preparing to protect exposures. When conditions allow, initiate an aggressive offensive attack at the main seat of the fire, but notify the Branch Director prior to commencing any offensive fire suppression actions. Monitor water supply. Provide the Branch Director with an update on current operations and results by 1200. Immediately report any changes in conditions.

8. SPECIAL INSTRUCTIONS

Safety: Take special precautions during night operations as conditions become much more hazardous and the chance for accidents increase. Use caution and avoid radiological contamination. All resources to sign the site safety plan prior to going on sift. Technical decontamination for responders is located at Elitch Circle Staging.

9. DIVISION/GROUP COMMUNICATIONS SUMMARY

FUNCTION		FREQ.	SYSTEM	CHAN.	FUNCTION		FREQ.	SYSTEM	CHAN.
COMMAND	LOCAL	CDF 1	King	1	SUPPORT	LOCAL			
	REPEAT					REPEAT			
DIV./GROUP TACTICAL		157.4505	King	3	GROUND TO AIR				

PREPARED BY (RESOURCES UNIT LEADER)	APPROVED BY (PLANNING SECT. CH.)	DATE	TIME
A. Worth 12 July 0300	J. Gafkjen	12 July	0330

"Example of a Specific ICS-204"

Example of a Branch Summary ICS-204

1. BRANCH Fire/Rescue	2. DIVISION/GROUP	**ASSIGNMENT LIST**	

3. INCIDENT NAME Denver RDD	4. OPERATIONAL PERIOD (Date and Time) 12 July 0600 to 12 July 1800

5. OPERATIONS PERSONNEL

OPERATIONS CHIEF_____B. Roberts_____ DIVISION/GROUP SUPERVISOR_____

BRANCH DIRECTOR_____R. Russell_____ AIR TACTICAL GROUP SUPERVISOR_____

6. RESOURCES ASSIGNED THIS PERIOD

STRIKE TEAM/TASK FORCE RESOURCE DESIGNATOR	EMT	LEADER	NUMBER PERSONS	TRANS NEEDED	DROP OFF POINT/TIME	PICK UP POINT/TIME
2 Fire Suppression TF						
2 Engine ST (Type 1)						
2 Police Units						
2 Ambulances (Type II)						
1 Air ambulance						
2 Heavy Rescue Companies						
2 Urban Search and Rescue TF						

7. ASSIGNMENT

* Fire Suppression Group to initiate aggressive offensive attack on main seat of fire both in the collapsed building and railroad cars
* Medical Group to continue triage, treatment, and transport of injured to local area hospitals
* Search and Rescue Group to apply all search techniques necessary to conduct searches in the damaged structures

8. SPECIAL INSTRUCTIONS

* Technical decontamination for responders is located at Elitch Circle Staging

* Fire/Rescue Branch Director cell phone # - 555-555-5555

9. DIVISION/GROUP COMMUNICATIONS SUMMARY

FUNCTION		FREQ.	SYSTEM	CHAN.	FUNCTION		FREQ.	SYSTEM	CHAN.
COMMAND	LOCAL REPEAT	CDF 1	King	1	SUPPORT	LOCAL REPEAT			
DIV./GROUP TACTICAL		157.4505	King	3	GROUND TO AIR				

PREPARED BY (RESOURCES UNIT LEADER) A. Worth 12 July 0300	APPROVED BY (PLANNING SECT. CH.) J. Gafkjen	DATE 12 July	TIME 0330

"Example of a Branch Summary ICS-204"

ICS FORMS LIST

Form	Title	Prepared By
ICS 201	Incident Briefing	Initial IC
ICS 202	Incident Objectives	PSC
ICS 203	Organization Assignment List	RESL
ICS 204	Assignment List	RESL, OSC, SOF, COML
ICS 205	Communications Plan	COML
ICS 206	Medical Plan	MEDL
ICS 207	Incident Organization Chart	RESL
ICS 209	Incident Status Summary	SITL
ICS 210	Status Change Card	On-scene incident dispatcher
ICS 211	Check-in List	RESL/ Check-in recorder
ICS 213	General Message	Any message originator
ICS 214	Unit Log	All Chiefs, Officers, Directors, Supervisors, Leaders
ICS 215	Operational Planning Worksheet	OSC
ICS 215a	IAP Safety Analysis	SOF
ICS 218	Support Vehicle Inventory	GSUL
ICS 219	Resource Status Card	RESL
ICS 220	Air Operations Summary Worksheet	OSC / AOBD
ICS 221	Demobilization Checkout	DMOB

Area Command Forms

Form	Title	Prepared By
ICS AC202-CG/EPA	Area Command Objectives	Planning Section Chief
ICS AC205a-CG/EPA	Area Command Communications List	Communications Unit Leader
ICS AC207-CG/EPA	Area Command Organization Chart	Resources Unit Leader
ICS AC209-CG/EPA	Area Command Status Summary	Situation Unit Leader
ICS AC215-CG/EPA	Critical Resource Allocation & Prioritization Worksheet	Command & Planning Section Chief
ICS AC230-CG/EPA	Area Command Daily Meeting Schedule	Situation Unit Leader

The US Coast Guard and Environmental Protection Agency Area Command Forms can be found at http://homeport.uscg.mil/mycg/portal/ep/home.do

Once at the website click on the tab marked Library. You will find a button on the left marked Incident Command System (ICS) that will take you to ICS Area Command forms.

GLOSSARY

---◆---

A

AGENCY EXECUTIVE — An individual from an agency, company or level of government to whom the member of the Unified Command from that agency or company reports during the response effort; may provide executive level direction to Command that influences the response effort.

AGENCY REPRESENTATIVE (AREP) — An individual assigned to an incident from an assisting or cooperating agency that has been delegated full authority to make decisions on all matters affecting their agency's participation at the incident. Agency Representatives report to the incident LOFR.

ALL-HAZARD — Any incident or event, natural or human caused, that requires an organized response by a public, private, and/or governmental entity in order to protect life, public health and safety, values to be protected, and to minimize any disruption of governmental, social, and economic services.

AREA COMMAND — An organization established to oversee the management of multiple incidents that are each being handled by an Incident Management Team (IMT). Area Command has the responsibility to set overall strategy and priorities, allocate critical resources according to priorities, ensure that incidents are properly managed, and ensure that objectives are met and strategies followed. (See also: Unified Area Command).

AREA OF RESPONSIBILITY — The domain within a specified set of boundaries, either geographic, functional or a combination thereof, for which you have been assigned incident management responsibility.

ASSIGNED RESOURCES — Resources checked in and assigned work tasks on an incident.

Assignments — Tasks given to resources to perform within a given operational period, based upon tactical objectives in the IAP.

Assistant — An ICS support position title for those personnel assigned to work for the Command Staff Officers e.g., Assistant Safety Officer. In some cases assistants may be assigned to support Unit Leaders.

Assisting Agency — An agency directly contributing or providing tactical or service resources to another agency.

Available Resources — Incident-based resources that are immediately available for assignment.

B

Base — That location at which the primary logistics functions are coordinated and administered. There is only one base per incident.

Branch — The organizational level having functional and/or geographic responsibility for major incident operations. The branch level is organizationally between section and division/group in the Operations Section and between section and units in the Logistics Section. Branches are identified by roman numerals or by functional name (e.g., Medical Branch).

C

Camp — Geographical site(s) within the general incident area, separate from the incident base, equipped and staffed to provide sleeping, food, water, and sanitary services to incident personnel.

Check-in — The process where responding resources let the Incident Commander (or incident management team) know they have arrived on-scene to support incident operations. Check-in can occur at five incident locations: Incident Command Post, Helibase, Staging Areas, Incident Base, and Camps.

CHIEF — The ICS title for individuals responsible for the command of functional sections: Operations, Planning, Logistics, and Finance/Administration.

COMMAND — The act of directing, ordering, and/or controlling resources by virtue of explicit legal, agency, or delegated authority. Also referred to as IC or UC.

COMMAND DIRECTION — A general term for the specific information provided by the IC/UC to the Command and General staff for action. Examples include priorities, objectives, tasks, policies, decisions and operating procedures.

COMMAND STAFF — The Command Staff consists of the PIO, SOF, and LOFR, who report directly to an IC. May also include Intelligence Officer. They may have assistants.

COMPLEX — Two or more individual incidents located in the same general proximity, which are assigned to a single IC or UC.

CONTINGENCY PLAN — The portion of an IAP or other plan that identifies possible but unlikely events and the resources needed to mitigate those events.

COOPERATING AGENCY — An agency supplying assistance other than direct tactical or support functions or resources to the incident control effort (e.g., Red Cross).

CRITICAL INCIDENT INFORMATION — Information that is of vital importance to officials who have a vested interest in the management of an Incident. Critical information must be reported immediately regardless of normal incident reporting cycles. Officials who have jurisdictional or functional responsibility over the incident normally determine what information is critical.

CRITICAL RESOURCE — A critical resource is when there is more demand for certain kinds of resources (e.g., specialized teams, personnel, or equipment), than there is available supply. The limited or unavailability of a critical resource will have a direct negative impact on the overall management of the incident.

D

DEMOBILIZATION — Release of resources from an incident in accordance with a detailed plan approved by the IC/UC.

DEPUTY — A fully qualified individual who, in the absence of a superior, could be delegated the authority to manage a functional operation or perform a specific task. In some cases, a deputy could act as relief for a superior and, therefore, must be fully qualified in the position. Deputies can be assigned to the Incident Commander, General Staff, and Branch Directors.

DIRECTOR — ICS title for individuals responsible for supervision of a branch.

DIVISION — Organization level used to divide an incident into geographical areas of operation. The division level is established when the number of resources exceeds the span-of-control of the OSC and is organizationally between the task force/strike team and the branch.

E

EMERGENCY OPERATIONS CENTER (EOC) — The pre-designated facility established by an agency or jurisdiction to coordinate the overall agency or jurisdictional response and support to an emergency. The EOC coordinates information and resources to support domestic incident management activities.

F

FINANCE/ADMINISTRATION SECTION — The section responsible for all administrative and financial considerations on an incident.

G

GENERAL STAFF — The General Staff is comprised of the following ICS positions: Operations Section Chief, Planning Section Chief, Logistics Section Chief, and Finance/Administration Section Chief. The General Staff reports directly to the Incident Commander/Unified Command.

GROUP — An organizational level established to divide the incident into functional areas of operation. Groups are composed of resources assembled to perform a special function not necessarily within a single geographic division.

H

HAND CREW — A number of individuals that have been organized and trained and are supervised for operational assignments on an incident.

HELIBASE — A location within the general incident area for parking, fueling, maintenance, and loading of helicopters.

HELISPOT — A location where a helicopter can take off and land. Some helispots may be used for temporary loading.

I

INCIDENT — An occurrence, either human-caused or natural phenomenon, that requires action or support by emergency service personnel to prevent or minimize loss of life or damage to property and/or natural resources.

INCIDENT ACTION PLAN (IAP) — An oral or written plan containing general objectives reflecting the overall strategy for managing an incident. It may include the identification of operational resources and assignments. It may also include attachments that provide direction and important information for management of the incident during one or more operational periods.

INCIDENT BASE — (see Base)

INCIDENT COMMANDER (IC) — The individual responsible for all incident activities, including the development of strategies and tactics and the ordering and release of resources. The IC has overall authority and responsibility for conducting incident operations and is responsible for the management of all incident operations at the incident site. (See also: Unified Command).

INCIDENT COMMAND POST (ICP) — The field location at which the primary tactical-level, on-scene incident command functions are performed. The ICP may be collocated with the incident base or other incident facilities.

INCIDENT COMMAND SYSTEM (ICS) — A standardized on-scene emergency management concept specifically designed to allow its user(s) to adopt an integrated organizational structure equal to the complexity and demands of single or multiple incidents, without being hindered by jurisdictional boundaries.

INCIDENT MANAGEMENT TEAM (IMT) — The Incident Commander and appropriate Command and General Staff personnel assigned to an incident.

INCIDENT OBJECTIVES — Statements of direction necessary for the selection of appropriate strategies, and the tactical direction of resources. Tactical incident objectives address the tactical response issues while management incident objectives address the incident management issues. Tactical incident objectives are based on realistic expectations of what can be accomplished when all allocated resources have been effectively deployed. Incident objectives must be achievable and measurable, yet flexible enough to allow for strategic and tactical alternatives.

INCIDENT PRIORITIES — Critical factors that influence the allocation of resources or actions necessary to achieve incident objectives, such as life safety, national security, environment, economy, infrastructure and transportation systems.

Incident Situation Display — The Situation Unit is responsible for maintaining a display of status boards, which communicate critical incident information vital to establishing an effective command and control environment.

Initial Action — The actions taken by the first resources to arrive at the incident. Initial actions may be to size up, patrol, monitor, withhold from any action, or take aggressive initial measures.

Interim Direction(s) — Specific tasking provided by Command to staff during periods of the response when more formalized direction has not yet been developed; the dynamics of the incident have suddenly changed; or at any other time Command deems necessary to fill gaps in their clarity of direction.

J

Joint Field Office (JFO) — A temporary federal facility established locally to provide a central point for federal, state, local, and tribal executives with responsibility for incident oversight, direction, and/or assistance to effectively coordinate protection, prevention, preparedness, response, and recovery actions.

Joint Information Center (JIC) — A facility established within or near the ICP where the PIO and staff can coordinate and provide information on the incident to the public, media, and other agencies.

Jurisdiction — The range or sphere of authority. Public agencies have jurisdiction at an incident related to their legal responsibilities and authority for incident mitigation. Jurisdictional authority at an incident can be political/geographical (e.g., city, county, state or federal boundary lines) or functional (e.g., police department, health department).

L

LEADER — The ICS title for an individual responsible for a task force/strike team or functional unit.

LIMITATIONS AND CONSTRAINTS — Influences that may hinder you from carrying out a planned action or something that may adversely affect how or when you can perform a task.

LOGISTICS SECTION — The Logistics Section is responsible for providing facilities, services, and materials in support of the incident.

M

MANAGEMENT BY OBJECTIVES — In ICS, this is a top-down management activity which involves the following steps to achieve the incident goal: (1) establishing incident objectives, (2) selection of appropriate strategy(s) to achieve the objectives, and (3) developing or identifying the tactical direction associated with the selected strategy.

MANAGERS — Individuals within ICS organizational units that are assigned specific managerial responsibilities (e.g., Staging Area Manager).

MESSAGE CENTER — The message center is part of the communications center and collocated with or adjacent to it. It receives, records, and routes information about resources reporting to the incident, resource status, and handles administration, and tactical traffic.

MULTI-AGENCY COORDINATION (MAC) — A generalized term which describes the functions and activities of representatives of involved agencies and/or jurisdictions who come together to make decisions regarding the prioritizing of incidents, and the sharing and use of critical resources. The MAC organization is not a part of the on-scene ICS and is not involved in developing incident strategy or tactics.

MULTI-AGENCY INCIDENT — Is an incident where one or more agencies assist a jurisdictional agency or agencies. There may be a single or Unified Command.

MULTI-JURISDICTIONAL INCIDENT — Is an incident requiring action from multiple agencies that each have jurisdiction to manage certain aspects of an incident. In ICS, these incidents will be managed under Unified Command.

N

NON-GOVERNMENTAL ORGANIZATION (NGO) — An entity that is based on interests of its members, individuals, or institutions and that is not created by a government, but may work cooperatively with government to serve a public purpose (e.g., faith-based charity organizations, American Red Cross).

O

OFFICER — The ICS title for personnel responsible for the Command Staff positions of Safety, Liaison, and Public Information.

ONGOING OPERATIONS — The period after the initial response phase; response activities are planned for in advance of the operational period when they will be executed. A continuous cycle of activities that result in development, execution, support and assessment of an Incident Action Plan. The cycle that continues until the incident is resolved.

OPERATIONAL PERIOD — The period of time scheduled for execution of a given set of operational actions as specified in the IAP. Operational periods can be various lengths, usually not over 24 hours. The operational period coincides with the completion of one planning cycle (see Chapter 3 planning cycle).

Operations Section — The section responsible for all operations directly applicable to the primary mission. Directs the preparation of branch, division, and/or unit operational plans, requests or releases resources, makes expedient changes to the IAP as necessary and reports such to the IC.

Out-of-Service Resources — Resources assigned to an incident, but are unable to respond for mechanical, rest, or personnel reasons.

Overhead Personnel — Personnel who are assigned to supervisory positions that include: Incident Commander, Command Staff, General Staff, Directors, Supervisors, and Unit Leaders.

P

Planning Section — The section that is responsible for the collection, evaluation, and dissemination of tactical information related to the incident, and for the preparation and documentation of Incident Action Plans. The section also maintains information on the current and forecasted situation, and on the status of resources checked-in to the incident.

R

Resources — General term of all personnel and major tactical equipment available or potentially available for assignment to an incident and for which status (assigned, available, out-of-service) is maintained.

Resource Allocation — The assigning of tactical resources to a particular incident(s) or to a division/group within the Operations Section.

Responder Rehabilitation — Also known as "rehab", a treatment of incident personnel who are suffering from the effects of strenuous work and/or extreme conditions.

S

Section — The ICS organization level having functional responsibility for primary segments of an incident such as: Operations, Planning, Logistics and Finance/Administration.

Single Resource — An individual piece of equipment with an identified work supervisor that can be used on an incident (e.g., ambulance, crane, dump truck).

Site Safety and Health Plan (SSHP) — Site-specific document required by state and federal OSHA regulations. SSHP following elements: health and safety hazard analysis for each site task or operation, comprehensive operations work plan, personnel training requirements, PPE selection criteria, site-specific occupational medical monitoring requirements, air monitoring plan, site control measures, confined space entry procedures (if needed), pre-entry briefings (e.g.,tailgate meetings), pre-operations commencement health and safety briefing for all incident participants, and quality assurance of SSHP effectiveness.

Situation Assessment — The evaluation and interpretation of information gathered from a variety of sources, including weather information and forecasts, computerized models, GIS data mapping, remote sensing sources, ground surveys, etc. This information, when communicated to emergency managers and decision makers, can provide a basis for incident management decision making.

Social Media — Use of online hardware and software communication technologies that enable individuals and/or groups to share audio, video, text and image information.

Span-of-Control — A command and control term that means how many organizational elements may be directly managed by one person. Span-of-control may vary from one to seven, and a ratio of five reporting elements is optimum.

Staging Area — That location where incident personnel and equipment are assigned awaiting tactical assignment. Staging Areas are in the Operations Section.

Stakeholders — Any person, group, or organization affected by and having a vested interest in the incident and/or the response operation.

Strategic Direction — The overarching plan or direction selected by high level officials to influence the overall accomplishments of a Incident Management Team.

Strategy — The general plan or direction selected to accomplish incident objectives.

Strike Team — Specified combinations of the same kind and type of resources with common communications and a leader.

Supervisor — ICS title for individuals responsible for command of a division or group.

T

Tactical Direction — Directions given by the OSC that include: the tactics appropriate for the selected strategy, the selection and assignment of resources, tactics implementation, and performance monitoring for each operational period.

Tactics — Deploying and directing resources during an incident to accomplish the objectives.

Task Force — A combination of different kinds of single resources that are assembled to accomplish a certain tactical assignment. For example, a Task Force may be comprised of a dump truck, excavator, and crane.

T-Card — Cards filled out with essential information for each resource they represent. The cards are color-coded to represent different kinds of resources.

Technical Specialists (THSP) — Personnel with special skills who can be used anywhere within the ICS organization.

U

Unified Command (UC) — An application of ICS used when there is more than one agency with incident jurisdiction or when incidents cross political jurisdictions. Agencies work together through the designated members of the Unified Command to establish a common set of objectives and strategies and a single Incident Action Plan. This is accomplished without losing or abdicating authority, responsibility, or accountability.

Unified Area Command (UAC) — A Unified Area Command is established when incidents under an Area Command are multi-jurisdictional.

Unit — That organizational element having functional responsibility for a specific incident planning, logistics, or finance/administration activity.

V

Volunteer — Any individual accepted to perform services by an agency that has authority to accept volunteer services when the individual performs services without promise, expectation, or receipt of compensation for services performed.

ACRONYMS

A

AC — Area Command
AOBD — Air Operations Branch Director
AREP — Agency Representative
ASGS — Air Support Group Supervisor
ATGS — Air Tactical Group Supervisor

B

BCMG — Base Manager

C

CLMS — Claims Specialist
COML — Communications Unit Leader
COMP — Compensation/Claims Unit Leader
COST — Cost Unit Leader

D

DIVS — Division/Group Supervisor
DMOB — Demobilization Unit Leader
DOCL — Documentation Unit Leader
DOSC — Deputy Operations Section Chief
DPRO — Display Processor

E

EOC — Emergency Operations Center
EQPM — Equipment Manager
EQTR — Equipment Time Recorder

F

FACL — Facilities Unit Leader
FDUL — Food Unit Leader

G

GSUL — Ground Support Unit Leader

I

IAP — Incident Action Plan
IC — Incident Commander
ICP — Incident Command Post
ICS — Incident Command System
INCM — Incident Dispatcher
INJR — Compensation for Injury Specialist

J

JFO — Joint Field Office
JIC — Joint Information Center

L

LOFR — Liaison Officer
LSC — Logistics Section Chief

M

MEDL — Medical Unit Leader

O

OPBD — Operations Branch Director
ORDM — Ordering Manager
OSC — Operations Section Chief

P

PIO — Public Information Officer
PROC — Procurement Unit Leader
PSC — Planning Section Chief
PTRC — Personnel Time Recorder

R

RCDM — Receiving and Distribution Manager

REHB — Responder Rehabilitation Manager

RESL — Resources Unit Leader

S

SCKN — Status/Check-In Recorder

SECM — Security Manager

SITL — Situation Unit Leader

SOF — Safety Officer

SPUL — Supply Unit Leader

SSHP — Site Safety and Health Plan

STAM — Staging Area Manager

STCR — Strike Team Leader

SUBD — Support Branch Director

SVBD — Service Branch Director

T

TFLD — Task Force Leader

THSP — Technical Specialist

TIME — Time Unit Leader

U

UAC — Unified Area Command

UC — Unified Command

NOTES

NOTES

Authors

Tim Deal — is the Federal Preparedness Coordinator for the Federal Emergency Management Agency (FEMA) in Region VIII. Prior to coming to FEMA he worked as Vice President in the emergency management training field. He has extensive emergency response experience serving in several ICS positions, including Planning Section Chief and Operations Section Chief.

Chuck Mills — is the President of Emergency Management Services International, Inc. He has more than 40 years experience in emergency management and provides emergency management services to government and non-governmental organizations. Chuck served 32 years in the US Forest Service, specializing in emergency management. He was the Federal representative for the development and implementation of the National Interagency Incident Management System Incident Command System.

Mike Deal — enjoyed a long career with AT&T as a Data Network Engineer, Instructor and Course Developer. That experience led to direct involvement with the design and layout of the authors' very successful previous book: "Beyond Initial Response" and now the "All Hazard Field Guide."

Made in the USA
Middletown, DE
01 March 2018